Visualizing Black Lives

Visualizing Black Lives

Ownership and Control in Afro-Brazilian Media

REIGHAN GILLAM

Urbana, Chicago, and Springfield

© 2022 by the Board of Trustees
of the University of Illinois
All rights reserved
1 2 3 4 5 C P 5 4 3 2 1
♾ This book is printed on acid-free paper.

Publication supported by a grant from the University
of Illinois Press Fund for Anthropology.

Library of Congress Cataloging-in-Publication Data
Names: Gillam, Reighan, author.
Title: Visualizing Black lives : ownership and control in
    Afro-Brazilian media / Reighan Gillam.
Description: Urbana : University of Illinois Press, [2022] |
    Includes bibliographical references and index.
Identifiers: LCCN 2021046191 (print) | LCCN 2021046192
    (ebook) | ISBN 9780252044410 (cloth) | ISBN
    9780252086489 (paperback) | ISBN 9780252053405
    (ebook)
Subjects: LCSH: Blacks and mass media—Brazil. | Blacks
    in mass media. | Racism in mass media. | Brazil—Race
    relations.
Classification: LCC P94.5.B552 B645 2022 (print) |
    LCC P94.5.B552 (ebook) | DDC 305.896/081—dc23/
    eng/20211202
LC record available at https://lccn.loc.gov/2021046191
LC ebook record available at https://lccn.loc.gov/2021046192

For my parents, Warren and Dorothy Gillam

Contents

Acknowledgments ix

Introduction 1

1 Mediating Resistance: Afro-Brazilian
  Media and Movements 17

2 TV da Gente and Controlling the Means
  of Media Production 31

3 Animating Racism: Irony and Images
  of Dissent 53

4 Independent Lenses: Learning to See
  in Afro-Brazilian Film 75

Conclusion: Antiracist Visual Politics 103

Notes 109

Works Cited 117

Index 133

Acknowledgments

After years of researching and writing this book, I am happy to finally thank in print those who supported my journey. I am indebted to the people in Brazil who shared their lives and experiences with me. They welcomed me and agreed to help me by sharing their stories and recollections, as well as the media that they made. This research and book would not be possible without their insights and words.

The seeds for this project were planted while I was an undergraduate at the University of Virginia. Classes with Brian Owensby, David Haberly, and Mieka Brand Polanco introduced me to the African Diaspora and the history and culture of Brazil. Hanan Sabea and Wende Marshall provided mentorship, advice, and models for infusing academic work with social justice. The Institute for the Recruitment of Teachers greatly aided my transition from college to graduate school.

I had the good fortune of learning in community at Cornell University and in the Department of Anthropology. Viranjini Munasinghe first told me about TV da Gente, guided my project development, and instilled in me an appreciation for irony. I am thankful to have had guidance building my project from Jane Fajans, Carol Boyce Davies, Dominic Boyer, Audra Simpson, and Jacob Rigi. The late John Burdick kindly met with me in Syracuse to offer advice about my research. I truly enjoyed Jurandir Oliveira's Portuguese classes and his exuberant teaching style. A class and discussions with Micol Seigel contributed to my thinking about this book and planted seeds for future projects. My cohort of Ivan Small, Kate Harding, Krista Schoening, Olivia Hall, and Hong Bui provided camaraderie during out journey through graduate school. I am grateful for Ivan's friendship as we navigate academia and life one conference at a time. Tina Shrestha, Bernardo Brown, John Phan, and Nidhi Mahajan have been friends and sources of support in graduate school and beyond. A Five College Fellowship at Mount Holyoke College gave me the needed time and space to write my dissertation. While there, Joshua Roth, Debbora Battaglia, Britt Halvorson, and my students made my experience of life at the college quite enjoyable.

My colleagues at the University of Michigan and at the University of Southern California have provided intellectually stimulating environments and community. I am grateful for those who supported me, including Tiya Miles, Martha Jones, Frieda Ekotto, Meg Sweeney, Aswin Punathambekar, Robin Means Coleman, Susan Douglas, Yeidy Rivero, Nayan Shah, Dorinne Kondo, and Shazia Iftkhar. The late Fernando Arenas helped me improve my Portuguese and offered constant support and advice for the project. May he rest in peace. Katherine Sender read through manuscript chapters and offered invaluable comments and advice. At Michigan, I was involved with the Program for Research on Black Americans (PRBA) as well as the Women of Color in the Academy Project (WOCAP). Writing retreats with WOCAP and presentations at PRBA helped me to advance this book. I am grateful to have had been in community with William Calvo-Quirós, Aliyah Khan, and Kira Thurman at Michigan. At USC Nancy Lutkehaus and Lanita Jacobs kindly read chapter drafts and offered advice. Deborah Thomas and Joseph Straubhaar offered incisive readings of the entire manuscript. These thoughtful critiques and questions helped me to refine this book. Through writing groups, reading groups, and other gatherings throughout my time in LA, I am thankful to have gotten to know Natalie Belisle, Kirby Farah, Xochitl Ruiz, Emily Zeamer, Adrian de Leon, Alaina Morgan, Ronald Mendoza de Jesus, and Zakkiyah Iman Jackson.

The David Rockefeller Center for Latin American Studies (DRCLAS) at Harvard University gave me the time and space needed to revise the manuscript. I enjoyed gathering with the other fellows and benefited from their questions and advice, especially Rosemary Feal and Flávia Piovesan. Edwin Ortiz ensured that our time at DRCLAS was productive and comfortable. Jessica Welburn, Matthew Morrison, Christopher Ouma, ZZ Packer, and I met regularly to write, which contributed to my revising momentum. M. Gabriela Torres and Amy Moran-Thomas offered comments on a chapter that I presented at the anthropology working group that Ieva Jusionyte coordinated. I am grateful for the fellowship with Todne Thomas and N. Fadeke Castor in Cambridge.

The book benefited from comments and questions from audiences at talks at Brown University, Harvard University, University of Pennsylvania,

University of Rochester, University of New Orleans, University College of London, Waseda University (Japan), the Role of Place in African American Autobiography NEH Institute, and the African Centered Cultural Expression NEH Institute.

I am grateful to my fellow Brazilianists who have offered comments on the work at conferences and during conversations: Gladys Mitchell-Walthour, Tianna Paschel, Kia Lilly Caldwell, Bryan Pitts, Jay Sosa, Aiala Levy, Daniel Gough, Jasmine Mitchell, Jonathan Square, Bryce Henson, Kim Butler, and Jaira Harrington. For their help and camaraderie in Brazil, I thank Marcio Macedo and Gabriela Watson-Burkett. Leticia Stanchi Pereira, Domênica Oliveira, and Roseangela Malachias offered me the gift of friendship during my fieldwork, for which I am truly grateful.

I remain grateful for the friendships of Elizabeth Hinton, Jennifer Eaglin, Deniqua Crichlow, Martin Fischoff, Mike Henry, Walter Middlebrooks, and Colleen MacNett, my oldest friend. They help me forget about work and enjoy life.

At the University of Illinois Press, Marika Cristofides believed in the project from the beginning and expertly shepherded the manuscript through review. Dawn Durante adeptly picked up the project after Marika's departure, and Alison Syring Bassford's capable hands saw the project through to the end. I thank the anonymous reviewers, whose comments further improved this book.

My family has been a source of constant support as they have patiently watched me complete this book. My parents, Warren and Dorothy Gillam, were my first teachers, and to them I owe everything. I am grateful for my aunts and cousins, whose care has sustained me throughout my life. The Curry family has offered constant support and encouragement during this long journey. Milton S. F. Curry has been a steadfast partner in all things, and your constant optimism keeps me going.

Introduction

On a hot day in July 2013, I accompanied Érico, his wife Kenia, and their children Mateus and Gabriela as they filmed a scene for their YouTube show, *Tá Bom Pra Você?* (Is that OK with you?), a series of videos that draw attention to and critique racial dynamics in Brazil. I had seen their videos after a friend shared them through social media. A friend of my friend put me in contact with the team, who agreed to meet with me. After having to cancel other meeting dates due to large-scale city events in Rio de Janeiro, I finally had the opportunity to talk with them about their videos. Expecting only to do an interview, I was surprised and delighted that Sunday to witness the team filming a scene on the street. Their daughter, Gabriela, donned a blonde wig, a blouse, and skirt. Érico cued her to walk toward the camera talking on her cell phone. She then looked up, appeared frightened, turned around, and ran. They did another take. After fixing Gabriela's shirt and brushing her wig straight, her mother, Kenia, took her to stand in the shade to avoid the heat of the day.

After the take met the director's approval, we began walking to shoot another scene. Érico then explained to me the premise of the episode, which would appear on their YouTube channel. Gabriela was playing a white woman walking along and talking on her cell phone. She sees two Black men (played by Érico and his son) talking, they look at her, and she gets scared. She takes off running in the opposite direction. The two Black men are actually undercover police officers who consider her suspicious for running. They chase her, catch her, and wind up arresting her. The scene presents two cases of mistaken identity: the white woman assumes the Black men are criminals, prompting her to run away, and the Black male police officers assume she is a suspect due to her behavior. At the end of the scenario, the two cops arrest her for the crime of racism.[1]

This book closely attends to the *Tá Bom Pra Você?* YouTube show and a broader set of media projects developed by Afro-Brazilians in southeastern Brazil to examine how they foreground issues of racism and centralize Black characters, themes infrequently found in mainstream media.[2] I argue that these media projects are sites of what I call *antiracist visual politics*, which describes the ways in media producers and the visual media they create identify, challenge, or break with racist practices, ideologies, and structures. In *Tá Bom Pra Você?*, the episode "Atitude Suspeita" (Suspicious attitude) names the suspicion of Black men as racism, by showing the undercover police officers chasing the perpetrator and arresting her at the end of the narrative. Érico created the scenario enacted above to draw attention to the stereotype of Black men as criminals and to depict how "Black citizens are perceived as potential disturbances to the social order" (Adorno 1996: 283). The scenario communicated the overall message that assuming that Black men are criminals is itself an act of racism. They remind audiences that racism is a crime in Brazil, although few are arrested for transgressing that law. Antiracist visual politics are enacted through, but not limited to, calling into question who controls media production, what meanings are associated with Blackness, and how racism is represented. In what follows, I examine how media producers, who are generally excluded from mainstream media, assert the right to control the means of representation through their own visual culture production.

Black activists and their allies in Brazil have managed to shift the terms of recognizing and redressing racism through political protests, demands for policies to facilitate Black inclusion, and everyday actions of consciousness raising. The government has implemented policies, such as affirmative action to increase access to higher education for Black and poor Brazilians. However, these social policies and the Black inclusion that they mandate have yet to trickle into images of Blackness in the mainstream media, which continues to be dominated by whiteness and stereotypical notions of Blackness. Afro-Brazilian media can be considered alternative in that it is "produced outside mainstream media institutions and networks" (Atton and Couldry 2003: 579).[3] By centering Afro-Brazilians and their life experiences, Afro-Brazilian media is alternative in that it expresses "an alternative vision to hegemonic policies, priorities, and perspectives" (Downing 2001: v). Yet, if we dismiss this media for its audience reach, we miss the opportunity to examine what kinds of images do antiracist work and how. Rather than simply create images, Black media producers discussed in this book challenge stereotypes and

Black invisibility as well as call for representational changes in the ways Black people are depicted. In this way, Afro-Brazilian visual culture production highlights the importance of media in the movement for Black inclusion. Afro-Brazilian media producers create visual images that offer new possibilities for representing Black subjectivities and they present images that contribute to antiracist activism and perspectives.

Representing Racism

That racism is represented in the media and how matters in a context where racism has been denied, downplayed, or left undefined. Traditional understandings of Brazil as a racial democracy have historically veiled experiences of racial difference and racism.[4] Brazil was known internationally as a racial democracy where many believed "that there has always been intimacy between whites and people of color rather than distance, that most Brazilians are 'racially mixed,' and that Brazil is relatively free of the racialized forms of prejudice and discrimination that plague countries such as the United States" (Sheriff 2000: 116).[5] Pervasive silences tamp down discussions of racism, such as when people are discouraged from recounting experiences of racism or when others deny that a given experience of exclusion can be defined as racism (Twine 1998; Sheriff 2000; Caldwell 2007). While the question of how racism is represented has implications outside of Brazil, it specifically addresses the particularities of racism in Brazil. Racial democracy has functioned as an "official, mythological anti-racism" by deeming the country free from racial distinctions and racism (Guimarães 1995: 225). Rosana Heringer notes that, given the context, "racism in Brazil must be given visibility" due to the general difficulty that people have in identifying its complex contours and workings (1995: 206). Afro-Brazilian media producers contribute to racial justice by exposing the dynamics of racism in its myriad forms. In this book, rather than evaluate the relationship between antiracism and media through media effects or changing public attitudes, I argue that the ways in which Afro-Brazilians lift the veil around racism challenges traditional representations of racism through their media interventions.

Racism is a persistent theme here and perhaps one of the most salient problems Afro-Brazilian media producers contend with through the themes in their media. It is clear that inequality does fall along racial lines (N. Silva 1985; Lovell 1999; Paixão 2004; Telles 2004) and that histories of enslavement and labor market exclusion have generated social and economic repercussions that continue to reverberate through contemporary Brazil in, for example, the concentration of people of African descent in the lowest economic categories

(Hasenbalg 1985; Bucciferro 2017). Afro-Brazilians also suffer from higher levels of police brutality and death from police violence (M. Mitchell and Wood 1999; Cano 2010; Smith 2016; Alves 2018), land dispossession (Perry 2013; Farfán Santos 2016), and lower health outcomes (Caldwell 2017), and they are underrepresented in every level of government in relation to their population size (Johnson 1998; Mitchell-Walthour 2017). Edward Telles identifies a "racist culture" in Brazil that is "based on a web of beliefs that subordinate positions are the proper place for browns and Blacks and that social spaces that involve control and access to resources should be occupied by whites" (2004: 222). This racist culture further undergirds, maintains, and normalizes the marginalization of Afro-Brazilians.

Despite research findings regarding racism, the topic emerges in mainstream media in limited ways. Often racism is named and made explicit through one-on-one interactions and appears as a result of ignorance or regressive attitudes. The telenovela *Duas Caras* (Two faces) ran from 2007 to 2008 during one of my research periods and presented racism as a narrative theme throughout the plot and a social problem to draw attention to. Samantha Nogueira Joyce (2012) describes one scene of explicit racism described by when a white female character, Júlia (Débora Falabella), invites a Black man, Evilásio Caó (Lázaro Ramos), to the home of her wealthy family for dinner. The telenovela *Duas Caras* explicitly depicts racism in a particularly explosive scene between Barreto (Sténio Garcia), Júlia's father and Evilásio. Barreto asks Evilásio for his opinion about the expensive wine they are drinking, possibly attempting to humiliate Evilásio. Evilásio replies that the wine tastes like "hot asphalt mixed with cigar" (Joyce 2012: 93). Júlia and another dinner guest laugh, but Evilásio's comments anger Barreto, who jumps up and calls Evilásio a "cocky *crioulo*," which is a racist expression. Júlia and her mother, Gioconda (Marília Pêra), asked Barreto to apologize to Evilásio and the other guests, which he refuses to do. Barreto says that Evilásio should apologize for exposing everyone to his type of person. Barreto responds, "imagine that: Paulo de Queiroz Barreto asking the forgiveness of a *tição*" (Joyce 2012: 94). A *tição* is an unmentionable racial slur in Brazil. This representation of racism through racial insult confines it to the problem of the racist individual, leaving those who do not demonstrate such behavior off the hook, and it prohibits understanding racism as a system that reaches beyond the individual. However, even this scene constitutes a departure from what scholars have found as the mainstream media's tendency to emphasize interracial harmony and omit topics of race and racism all together (De Lima 1996–97; Leslie 1999; Ramos 2002; J. Araújo 2002; Heise 2012; Rosas-Moreno 2014).

The ways in which media, particularly television and telenovelas, depicts social problems is important due to its centrality in elaborating meanings associated with the national imagination (Martín-Barbero 1993). Miguel Sabido developed and implemented the idea of entertainment-education to present media messages in telenovelas that address social problems, create social norms, and change behavior (Rosas-Moreno 2017). For example, Brazilian telenovelas have been shown to contribute to reducing family sizes by presenting representations of families with numbers of children that fell below the norm during the late 1970s and 1980s (La Ferrara, Chong, and Duryea 2012). Analyses point to the "image of the families—what has been shown rather than talked about—that has been adopted" (Rosas-Moreno 2014: 31). Given the power of the media in raising awareness of social problems and promoting social change, that they leave intact understandings of racism largely through individual interactions does a disservice to antiracist politics. It is important to understand racism in its various manifestations in order to work toward dismantling it.

Afro-Brazilian media producers harness the power of the media to introduce new and different representations of racism and racial inequality. In this media, both everyday and structural racism take center stage through the depiction of characters confronting racism in the area of aesthetics, everyday interactions, and structural forms. During interviews, producers revealed the ways in which they drew from their own interactions with and understandings of racism to tell stories about Black people rooted in the everyday conditions of their lives. They emphasize depictions of structural forms of racism or "any sort of hierarchical classification or justification of the domination, privileges and material and symbolic inequalities between human beings based on the imaginary concept of race and the arbitrary choice of bodily traits. From a social and economic standpoint, this hierarchical classification is expressed by practices that uphold an unequal opportunity structure and perpetuate the presence of a given group in lower strata of social indicators, with unequal access to employment, salaries, education, safety etc." (Machado, Santos and Ferreira 2015: 63). Chapters 3 and 4 emphasize how media and visual culture render the mechanisms through which the world presents Afro-Brazilians as nonnormative. They also show a pattern in interactions whereby Black people are interpolated through stereotypes in everyday life. In Afro-Brazilian media, racism emerges as more than a manifestation of interpersonal interactions; instead, it is embedded within the very structures and institutions that contextualize social life.

Leith Mullings's research is instructive for understanding the work of antiracism. Afro-Brazilian media demonstrates the antiracist work media can do by depicting "the hidden transcripts of the process through which difference is transformed into inequality" (Mullings 2005: 685). To show how Blackness becomes subject to unequal conditions is the visual work of antiracism. The "Atitude Suspeita" episode demonstrates this process through the encounter between a white woman and Black shoppers. When she sees them, reacts in fright, points, and runs the other way, calling the police, their racial difference becomes a marker of an assumed criminal status. Other Afro-Brazilian media present this process through various forms, including during everyday encounters, through national ideologies, and hegemonic structures. To insist on representing racism is to acknowledge their social realities and denaturalize the everyday conditions that structure Black lives.

In many ways, the diverse projects by contemporary Black media producers engage and adapt the performances undertaken by Afro–Latin Americans to assert their agency, challenge racism, and creatively express themselves. For example, Javier Cardona contests anti-Black racism in Puerto Rico through his theater performance of *You Don't Look Like* by illuminating the roles available to him as a Black actor and more generally the roles that Black Puerto Ricans are expected to inhabit (Rivero 2006). Additionally, the acting troupe *Choque Cultural* (Culture shock) disrupts the silence that obscures the violence of Brazilian racism by enacting scenes of encounters with the police in their public performances in Salvador, Bahia (Smith 2016). Critical attention by Yeidy Rivero and Christen Smith to the ways in which Afro–Latin Americans enlist performance to reveal how anti-Blackness operates and denounce it has established a strong foundation for continued investigations into the relationship between expressive cultural production and antiracism. This book analyzes media and visual culture to argue that the antiracist work that media can do includes how Afro-Brazilian producers marshal their own interpretations of racial dynamics and Black identity to critique mainstream media.

Who Controls the Means of Media Production?

By centering the perspectives of Black media producers, *Visualizing Black Lives* contributes to scholarship on race, Blackness, and representation in the Brazilian media. This body of research primarily employs textual analysis of mainstream media programs to excavate the ways in which these texts resist, uphold, or negotiate ideologies; this research grounds the text within their particular historical, social, or cultural context. This method and body of work has been critical to describing the ways in which the mass media in Brazil perpetuates stereotypes of Afro-Brazilians and further buttresses racism. Yet, the views and interpretations of the producers, particularly Black producers, have received little attention. The area of media production studies has revealed the importance of the practices and cultures of media producers (Mayer, Banks, and Caldwell 2009), which this book builds on by empirically documenting the perspectives, experiences, and ideas of Afro-Brazilian media producers. How do Afro-Brazilian media producers channel the intentions and imperatives of antiracist struggles in Brazil?

Afro-Brazilians producing their own media asserts their right to participate in and have control over the means of representation. Minoritized and subaltern communities and individuals constitute media as a site of struggle as they turn to the practice of creating their own media as an act of self-determination, cultural preservation, or, in the case of many Indigenous people, sovereignty. Anthropological studies of subaltern media have been preoccupied with Indigenous media, and they have demonstrated how media technologies of dominant societies provide the means through which Indigenous communities preserve and present their own cultural practices (Ginsburg 1991, 1997; Turner 1992, 2002; Wortham 2013). I draw from and contribute to this work, while shifting the lens to focus on the ways in which Afro-Brazilians use media to channel antiracist struggle. This question of who participates in media production is not necessarily new. Yet, it is critical in Brazil, where Afro-Brazilians are disproportionately underrepresented in the ranks of film and media workers (Candido et al. 2014). For example, Afro-Brazilians comprise 2 percent of film directors who had a commercially released film (14). Media producers shape the country's image of itself, which links to who belongs in the national polity and who the category of citizen includes (Baez 2018). As Afro-Brazilians have been distanced from the means of representation, their calls for inclusion in media production name the exclusion of Black media producers as a problem and their acts of producing their own media assert the importance of their presence in visual culture and media production, which, I argue, participates in the work of antiracist visual politics.

While the issue of who gains the opportunity to produce media is important, the question of control also has salience. As media producers exert important influence over the shape and message of media images (Dornfeld 1998), minoritized media producers can significantly change the texture and feel of images of their communities when they gain the access and ability to control the means of representation (Gray 1995). Many of the media producers I discuss had experience working in mainstream media, yet they lacked the ability to inject their ideas and increase Black representation in many of their jobs. In chapters 1 and 2, I focus on media producers who identify as Black and examine how they negotiate unequal media systems and institutions through protesting and critiquing dominant images, working from within mainstream media, and producing their own content. I contend that the actions of developing and organizing independent Black media should be seen as acts that call into question which narratives about race and Black identity can be told in Brazil; further, it asserts the right for Afro-Brazilians to participate in the production of meaning in general media texts as well as in ascribing meanings to their own identities.

Meanings Associated with Blackness

Afro-Brazilian media producers expand the arena of antiracist struggles to target the mass media as a site of ongoing exclusion and erasure. As elsewhere in Latin America, such as in Puerto Rico (Rivero 2005; Godreau 2008) and Colombia (Rivero 2014), the mainstream media in Brazil has not represented the depth and breadth of Black lives. The problems inherent to Black representation include casts that underrepresent Afro-Brazilians in relation to their population size, the ongoing patterns of stereotypical roles, and a general lack of attention to racism and racial inequality. Also, Afro-Brazilians are rarely the stars or central protagonists of programs. Academics have found that the narratives and messages of telenovelas, as well as the characters that Afro-Brazilians play, constitute mainstream media images as sites of racial inequality (De Lima 1988; Costa 1989; Sódre 1999; De Lima 2000–2001; Ramos 2002; J. Araújo 2006; Tavares 2010; Soares 2012; D. Oliveira 2014). The Multidisciplinary Studies of Affirmative Action Group at the Rio de Janeiro State University found that between 1995 and 2014, only 10 percent of the actors in telenovelas were Black or brown (Campos, Candido, and Feres Júnior 2014),[6] while according to the 2010 census, over 50 percent of Brazilians identified as nonwhite, which demonstrates an unequal pattern of representation.[7] Liv Sovik argues that the dominance of whiteness in the media is linked to past projects of whitening, or *branqueamento*, where "whiteness continues to be a project for the nation, a positive self image" (2004: 315).

The dominant "regime of racial representation" in mainstream media includes a series of representational and discursive practices that signify racial difference and confer specific meanings onto Blackness in the form of stereotypes (Hall 1997). In his study of Brazilian telenovelas, titled *A Negação do Brasil* (Denying Brazil), Joel Zito Araújo (2000) undertook an extensive content analysis of representations of Afro-Brazilians in telenovelas from the 1960s until the 1990s and defined the typology of roles that Afro-Brazilian actors primarily played as maids, butlers, and loyal and obedient enslaved people. Similarly, João Carlos Rodrigues (1988) identified a number of stereotypes or archetypes related to Afro-Brazilians in films.[8] To Rodrigues's list of archetypes, Candido and Feres Júnior (2019) analyzed a selection of feature-length films from 2002 to 2014 and found that Black women appear through such stereotypes as the favela woman, maid, or evangelical. In addition to showing Afro-Brazilian characters in the context of plantation life or in service positions, television and cinema have incorporated them into representations of favela life. Favelas are unplanned communities of informal housing in many Brazilian cities, such as on the outskirts of São Paulo or in the hills of Rio de Janeiro. *Cidade de Deus* (2001, *City of God*), the internationally renowned, Oscar-nominated film, popularized this representation by portraying the violence of favela life resulting from drug wars. Jaime Alves argues that *Cidade de Deus* paints a picture of Black manhood and boyhood as "synonymous with violence, virility, savagery" due to the constant violence enacted by young, Black male characters (Alves 2014: 317). The television microseries *Subúrbia* (2012) continues to misrepresent Afro-Brazilians through stereotypes and remains "silent with regard to the socioeconomic and racial inequalities that characterize the marginalized spaces it is increasingly representing" (Carter 2018a: 234). Television and cinema represent Afro-Brazilians as poor and marginal without attending to the inequalities that shape their experiences, thus naturalizing their position as marginal.[9]

Moving beyond the discussion of stereotypes, other problems with Black representation abound. Some films that include Black characters contain Afro-Brazilian culture within folkloric, premodern, or romanticized categories (Stam 1997). These representations fail to address contemporary racism or "the ordinary struggles of everyday Black Brazilians" in favor of Afro-Brazilians engaged in practices such as Candomblé and Carnaval (Stam 1997: 338). In an examination of more recent films, released between 1995 and 2010, Tatiana Heise (2012) shows that discussions of race and racial inequality are muted. Stam finds that "the most striking absence within Brazilian cinema is that of the Black woman" (Stam 1997: 342). Black male characters tend to enter into relationships with white women, and adaptations of stories with Black mixed-race characters are often played by white actresses. Also relatively absent are Black gay and lesbian characters. Finally, Denise Ferreira da Silva found that the problem of Black characters on telenovelas is "that these characters have no psychological depth, as do the majority of the other characters who are 'white'" (1999: 349).

Some films and television shows demonstrate progress but continue similar problematic patterns. Analyzing Black characters in telenovelas from 2000 to 2010, Grijó and Sousa (2012) found some advances in representation, including a small number of Black protagonists and groups of Black characters. The film *Antônia* (2006) offers an articulation of "hip hop feminist politics" by presenting Afro-Brazilian women's voices, their challenges to and by patriarchy, and artistic expression through hip-hop (J. Mitchell 2009). Yet, Grijo and Sousa (2012) found a continuation of stereotypes regarding Black people, small numbers of Black characters, and the absence of racial conflict. Although television presents more roles for Black actors, Jasmine Mitchell found that images of mixed-Black female bodies during the 2000s in telenovelas managed Blackness by containing it to the sexual sphere or the past, which serves to "buttress white supremacy and discipline people of African descent" (2020: 4). While more Black characters are present in mainstream television, the composition of majority white casts persists. In 2013, the telenovela *Amor à Vida* (Trail of Lies) debuted without a single Black actor in the cast. This pattern repeated itself in 2018, when the telenovela *Segunda Sol* (A second chance) debuted with no Black actors in the first episode. The cast had three Black actors, but not in any main roles (Cowie 2018). To add insult to injury, *Segunda Sol* took place in Bahia, the state known as the center of Black culture in Brazil.

The harm of stereotypes, invisibility, and distorted representations of Afro-Brazilians lies in their support and reinforcement of established social and racial hierarchies. Representations that reduce Black "people to a few, simple, essential characteristics, which are represented as fixed by nature" (Hall 1997: 255), enact power as "a key element in this exercise of symbolic violence" (259). In casting Afro-Brazilians as an expendable population, these images justify their exclusion and the abuse enacted on them by the police and other state sanctioned forces. If media constitutes one of the central means of imagining the national community, then the absence or distortion of Afro-Brazilians indexes their lack of belonging (La Pastina, Straubhaar, and Sifuentes 2014). Tina Campt's assertion "that images matter to Black folks" resonates in Brazil, in that images "offer individuals in those communities a medium through which to create a vision of themselves that does not always square with how they are popularly perceived" (2012: 5). Many people of African descent understand that the media's distorted images of them contribute to the societal harm and systematic exclusion they experience, which can inform their attention to and deployment of media as a site for racial justice. There appears to be little room for critique or alternatives in the mainstream media, which makes media and visual culture produced by Afro-Brazilians a rich site for examining other possibilities for Black representation. What kinds of narratives do Afro-Brazilian media producers think need to be told? How do Afro-Brazilian media producers determine what kinds of stories to tell?

Afro-Brazilian media producers make their own images of complex Blackness, which, I argue, break from mainstream representations and demonstrate that other kinds of images are possible. While we know how to identify stereotypes, archetypes, and missing racial subject matter in mainstream media, the ineffable representation of complex Black humanity continues as a general demand of the mass media. Media studies scholars and anthropologists of media offer key insights regarding the ways that images of minoritized populations lack depth. Kristen Warner identifies "plastic representations" of minoritized characters in mainstream U.S. television as those that tend to lack depth, complexity, or multidimensionality and are concerned "with the quantity of difference rather than the dimensionality of those performances" (2017: 33). Other images may conform to "ideal types of monogamy, gender conformity, and social success" (Howe 2013: 146) or appear distant from the population's everyday realities (Dávila 2001: 124).

Afro-Brazilian media producers create media and visual culture that is rooted in a demand for images of Black subjects that emphasize their agency, multidimensionality, and the realities of life in a society structured by race. In her examination of theater, Dorinne Kondo warns that, in a dramatic structure centered on a singular protagonist or hero, "if the hero is white and masculine—the case of most mainstream narratives—we are deprived of a similar depth of knowledge about the conflicts and emotions of the subordinate characters" (2018: 120). Casting minoritized characters as protagonists can make their feelings and conflicts central to the story. Afro-Brazilian media present representations of Afro-Brazilians as protagonists and central subjects, or as "at once a product or agent of history; the site of experience, memory, storytelling and aesthetic judgment; an agent of knowing as much as action" (Beihl, Good, and Kleinman 2007: 14). Centralizing Black characters enables viewers to follow their journeys, remain attuned to their feelings and experiences, and understand their motivations. I attend to the ways in which media producers develop constructs of real people rooted in actual lives, which endows images and characters with subjective dimensions that communicate their humanity and complexity. If images of Blackness have been overdetermined from without, then gaining control over one's own image production, portraying Black subjects as central, and presenting images that are more faithful to the lives of those populations, contributes to an antiracist agenda by offering other possible images and asserting the right to produce meanings around their own identities (Fanon 1967). At stake in this endeavor is not to define the attributes of complex Black images, but rather to analyze the processes and products of those who are expanding the breadth and deepening the dimensions of Black representations while remaining conscious of the ways in which images intersect with power dynamics.

In addition to making Black subjects central, Afro-Brazilian media producers render Black protagonists in forms that differ from mainstream media. They introduce Black children and middle-class professionals as central subjects. While these subjects are agents, they experience and confront racism as they navigate the social world. Yet, they continue to pursue their ambitions and goals in spite of societal obstacles. Their narratives are infused with humor, self-discovery, persistence, and authority, which cast Black subjects in a different light than in dominant media. Afro-Brazilian producers create media that center Black protagonists and depict experiences that emerge from life in a society structured by race. Afro-Brazilian media is a site of "Black affirmation," which Hilda Lloréns defines as a countercurrent against whitening that "reflects a desire to maintain and affirm Blackness [and] stems from the value that many individuals and communities place on their identities and ways of life" (2018: 158). These images, found in chapters 2, 3, and 4, assert complex Black humanity as they break with mainstream images of Blackness and offer new and imaginative possibilities for representing Black subjects and their lived realities.

These attempts to visualize Black lives can easily be read either as cries for authenticity or as essentialist traps. I do not characterize all media produced by Afro-Brazilians nor every aspect of the media I include in this book as contributing to antiracist visual politics. In discussing Black theater, Ieda Martins warns against locating its distinction in "the color, phenotype or ethnicity of the dramaturge, actor, director, or of the subject that is staged" (1995: 26). I follow her in not essentializing Black productions through the racial identity of the people creating the piece or those appearing in the program. Martins asserts that, "when one anchors this color or phenotype, in the experience, memory and place of this subject, these elements are erected as signs that project and represent" (26). Thus, it is not the color of the producer or actor that signifies Blackness, but the context from which it emerges and in which it is placed. Afro-Brazilian media makers represent Black racial difference through attention to histories of slavery and ongoing conditions of dispossession, everyday and structural racism that constrain their lives, and contexts of exclusion that condition their turn toward Blackness.

Background

In order to examine the ways in which Afro-Brazilians developed their own media and the meanings it communicates, I undertook data collection through textual analysis, semi-structured interviews, and participant observation. I collected the data in this book over a period of a year in 2007 and

2008, and during shorter fieldwork trips in 2004, 2005, 2009, and 2013. I gathered media produced by Afro-Brazilians and subjected it to textual analysis to discern the meanings of a given text and how it reflects and/or challenges hegemonic beliefs and dominant ideologies around race. I placed this media in relation to other mainstream media programs at the time to compare and contrast their messages. The texts were interpreted within the context of Brazilian social and cultural understandings of race, racism, and Blackness at the time period of their development and distribution. I attended to what kinds of issues they included and how, in what ways they depicted racism, the challenges and opportunities that protagonists encountered, and how they dealt with stereotypes. I noted consistencies and variations in subject matter, symbolic meanings, and subversion of hegemonic racial constructs in drawing connections between different programs and images.

I combined textual analysis with interviews with thirty-one media producers to understand the creators' intentions, ideas, and inspiration. During interviews, I asked participants about their background in studying and working in media, their opinion of mainstream representations of Blackness, as well as why and how they produced their own media. Taking the textual analysis into account, I tailored specific questions to each producer around the decisions they made in developing their stories, casting roles, and choosing their themes and subject matter. I also asked about the challenges and triumphs of producing their own media. Interviews generally lasted from forty-five minutes to an hour, though I interviewed some people twice. They took place at people's homes, places of employment, and at public locations convenient for us to access. In naming research participants, I use pseudonyms unless the person asked me to use their given name or they are public figures.

Finally, participant observation allowed me to understand the conditions of media production, the producers themselves, and the broader context and communities in which they circulated. As with the *Tá Bom Pra Você?* YouTube series that opens the introduction, I accompanied producers when filming their programs. I also attended social events with participants, including presentations, theatrical shows, family gatherings, media screenings, and film release parties. These activities enabled me to place media producers within their networks of relations, hear reactions to their work, and understand the broader political scene in which they were enmeshed.

I was drawn to the city of São Paulo because it was the home of the TV da Gente network, the first television channel to include Black representation as part of its mission. From contacts within the network and word of mouth, I located other Black media producers making their own short films, videos, and illustrations that included a critique of racial dynamics. While

Salvador, Bahia, a city in northeastern Brazil, has the population with the largest percentage of people of African descent, São Paulo has the largest number of Black people.[10] Of São Paulo's twelve million residents, 32 percent identify as Black or brown (IGBE 2010), and the city has a thriving Black cultural and political scene. Regarding Black culture in São Paulo, sociologist Marcio Macedo (2007) identified a "Black circuit" of samba performances, Black dances, and hip-hop clubs in the old city center, where Afro-Brazilians of all ages gather to talk, flirt, drink, and dance. In São Paulo, Black and marginal youth created Brazilian hip-hop in the city's outskirts to give voice to their struggles and outlooks (Pardue 2008; Reiter and Mitchell 2008; Jacqueline Santos 2016). Afro-Brazilian evangelicals develop different meanings of Blackness through their performances of gospel rap, gospel samba, and Black gospel music (Burdick 2013). I interacted with research participants in various events associated with São Paulo's Black political and cultural scene. I attended meetings organized through the Secretaria Especial de Políticas para a Promoção da Igualdade Racial (Special Political Secretariat for the Promotion of Racial Equality), where leaders surveyed Black community groups about their concerns. I frequented events at the Museu AfroBrasil, in São Paulo's Parque Ibirapuera, which "documents, preserves and argues from the perspective and experience of Blacks on the formation of Brazilian identity" (E. Araújo 2015: 154). Participating in activities at these and other venues enabled me to gain an understanding of community perspectives and commitments as well as the local Black political context.

Book Organization

Chapter 1 situates Afro-Brazilian media historically through a discussion of Black protest and expressive cultural production. It presents an overview of Black struggles for improved social conditions, freedom, inclusion, and recognition in Brazil from slavery to the early twenty-first century. Protests that decried and denounced racism in the mainstream media and called for Afro-Brazilian inclusion in controlling image production emerge throughout the chapter to demonstrate that the struggle for Black people to tell their own stories is linked to a larger movement for full inclusion in Brazilian society. I argue that the activism directed toward the media does the work of denaturalizing the gaze by calling into question who represents Afro-Brazilians and how, as well as illuminating inequities in media production. Afro-Brazilian media and visual culture production's link to Black social movements conditions the emergence of antiracist visual politics.

Chapter 2 turns to the TV da Gente (Our TV) television network, the first channel in Brazil to embrace racial diversity as part of its mission. Issues of ownership and control emerge in discussing the network's founding and through comparison between workers' experiences in mainstream media and at TV da Gente. I argue that ownership and control over media production are central to antiracist visual politics by enabling those seeking social change to have a hand in creating representations. I examine how the producers take up the dimension of class by representing middle-class, professional Afro-Brazilians in programming as a source of inspiration for their intended audiences. The producers drew from their own networks and identities as Black professional workers to create images of Black success, professionalism, and authority. I argue that, by emphasizing middle-class professionals, they challenged the traditional notion that "money whitens," or that upward mobility allows one to exit the category of Blackness. By situating Black people as hosts of the various programs, the network presented an image of Afro-Brazilian control over the flow of programming. By asserting themselves as owners, producers, and authorities in media production, they demonstrate the importance of the presence of Afro-Brazilians in these spaces and right to represent themselves.

Chapter 3 analyzes images and videos that narrate experiences of structural and interpersonal racism in the *Tá Bom Pra Você?* YouTube series, the Urban Saci graffiti series, and the illustrations of Mauricio Pestana. I consider how and why the audiences and creators find humor in some of these images and scenarios that depict racism as it occurs and structures daily life. These images narrate racism to ironic effect, which I argue diverges from mainstream media's downplaying of racism and the national appropriation of Black culture. By depicting racism as they experience and observe it in everyday life, they call into question traditional narratives that deny the existence of racism. Also, animating their experiences with racism enables media producers to communicate the tensions, contradictions, and inconsistencies of living in a society where racism is both denied and a routine aspect of everyday life. I contend that they use humor and irony in new ways by shifting attention away from Afro-Brazilians as an object of ridicule to present life from a Black perspective and to turn the critical lens onto Brazilian society.

Chapter 4 takes a closer look at Afro-Brazilian film through an analysis of three short films, including *A Formação do Olhar* (The formation of looking), *Cores e Botas* (Colors and boots), and *Jennifer*. Access to the means of representation emerges where I position Afro-Brazilian cinema as a site of control over image production. The films feature Black children and adolescents and the racial dynamics of their worlds, which acknowledges the existence of Black children and casts them as central to racial politics. Specifically, they problematize Black children's exposure to media that does not visually include them. In so doing, the films depict racism by tracking the sight of their young Black protagonists and drawing a relation between the hegemonically white visual world that they witness and the children's own struggles to accept themselves as they are. These representations of racism attend to the ways in which anti-Blackness structures the visual world, thus moving beyond mainstream renderings of racism. Afro-Brazilian filmmakers materialize their own ideas and visions through the creation of these films and present learning to recognize racism as a critical dimension to coming of age.

The conclusion considers the general themes that emerge across all the media to assess the meanings the producers attribute to Blackness. It then turns briefly to the expansion and contraction in the area of Afro-Brazilian media and distribution. Throughout the book, the actions of Afro-Brazilian media producers point to how antiracism can be materialized in relation to media work, such as through including Afro-Brazilians in front of and behind the camera to an extent that reflects their population size, and through Afro-Brazilian creative control of narratives that address various forms of racism and move beyond the framework of individual blame and culpability, thus re-signifying the meanings conferred onto Blackness and taking into account the ways in which images maintain or challenge oppressive racial conditions and discourses. These are the first steps, but they are far from the only strategies, to produce images of Black freedom in a society that insists on Black subjugation.

1

Mediating Resistance
Afro-Brazilian Media and Movements

The Dia da Consciência Negra (Day of Black Consciousness) holiday and celebration in Brazil falls on November 20. On this day, Zumbi dos Palmares is said to have died defending the Palmares Quilombo from Portuguese attackers in 1695. Enslaved people who escaped formed *quilombos*, communities or settlements typically hidden in remote areas.[1] In São Paulo, November might also be considered Black consciousness month due to the proliferation of activities and events about Black history and culture. Throughout November 2007, I attended numerous lectures, debates, and discussions about topics regarding Afro-Brazilian and African history and culture. On November 20, I attended the Black Consciousness March on Avenida Paulista. Amid the crowd of marchers, contingents of protesters for affirmative action at the Universidade de São Paulo (University of São Paulo) chanted slogans of support and cultural groups such as *capoeira* practitioners demonstrated their moves as we moved along the avenue. Large trailers carried organizers using bullhorns to call out messages of solidarity and uplift through the masses of people. The recognition and celebration of the Dia da Consciência Negra as a holiday is just one outcome of Black resistance and organizing in Brazil. Black movement activists had called for establishing November 20 as the Dia da Consciência Negra to honor Zumbi as part of their demands for Black recognition and inclusion. The meaning of the day and its activities bring to the fore centuries of resistance on the part of Black people from slavery to the present day.

Afro-Brazilians have taken advantage of media technologies as they have become available during the twentieth and twenty-first centuries in order to document Black voices and experiences. This book focuses on Afro-Brazilian media producers I encountered during fieldwork from 2005 to 2013. This chapter contextualizes the media and media producers I examine as part of a larger field of Black media production with a deeper history of individual and collective Black movements for representation. These previous media and visual culture projects demonstrate actions of Afro-Brazilians producing their own media and representations that confer meanings onto Blackness that they control. These actions and the images they created establish a tradition of media and visual culture production rooted in Afro-Brazilian agency and antiracism.

This chapter offers a brief overview of moments in history when protest resulted in significant sociopolitical change. The racial regimes of domination that Afro-Brazilians struggled against include the institution of slavery, post-abolition European immigration and discrimination, and, after 1930, the ideology of racial democracy and continued racism. Protest has been foundational to establishing Blackness as a legible category of identity, demonstrating that racial inequality and racism exist, advocating for Black inclusion in Brazilian institutions, and affirming Black culture, people, and lives. While affirmative action and other educational policies have received attention as the center of Black politics, I argue that media and visual culture have been sites of racial struggle in Brazil. Race-related protest flows from organizations, NGOs, and individuals, who target the government, civil society, cultural institutions, and the hearts and minds of everyday people as sites of change.[2] Although in this chapter I focus only on large-scale events and recent political outcomes, individuals and small groups continue to work tirelessly along multiple fronts to valorize Blackness and improve the conditions of Black life. Also, while I aim my lens mainly toward southeastern Brazil, Black constituencies all over the country have maintained vigorous resistance and advocated for Black people.[3]

I argue that Afro-Brazilian media and the antiracist visual politics it engenders emerge from and facilitate Black movement activism. I examine how past media and visual culture projects align with Black activism as well as more recent and explicit interrogations of the racial logics embedded within mainstream media. These explicit interrogations take the form of government sponsored meetings and independent manifestos, which, I argue, are calls to "denaturalize the gaze conditioned by racism" (Ribeiro 2019: 32). Afro-Brazilian activist and philosopher Djamila Ribeiro asserts that "the absence or low incidence of Black people in spaces of power does not usually bother or surprise white people. To denaturalize this, *all* should question the absence of Black people in positions of management, Black authors in anthologies, Black thinkers in the bibliography of university courses, Black protagonists in audiovisual" (32). I include examples of efforts by Black Brazilians to challenge the hegemonic norms of media production and call for the inclusion of Blackness in public cultural expressions. In so doing, they contribute to a process of questioning the absence of Black media producers and the ways in which Blackness is represented. They extend Black activism to the visual realm by calling for consciousness around how many and how Black people do and do not appear in front of and behind the camera. Black media producers wage protests around representation alongside larger Black mobilizations for autonomy, inclusion, and recognition in Brazil. That they emerge from and contribute to Black activism is foundational to Black media and visual culture's formulation of antiracist visual politics.

Black Media and Visual Culture Foundations

Here I examine key moments of Black struggle and the media and visual culture that emerged in relation to these processes. Media and visual culture offered a space to materialize the political currents of the moment and an opportunity for Afro-Brazilians to present themselves in ways that they controlled. In Brazil, Black resistance to the condition of enslavement took many forms, including stopping or slowing down work, running away, and rebellions. Ultimately, enslaved and free Black people's movements played a critical role in the abolition of slavery. After a series of electoral reforms passed to slow the abolition of slavery during the 1870s and 1880s, radical abolitionists relied on civil disobedience and nonviolent strategies to bring about the end of slavery. Abolitionists circulated throughout the countryside of the state of São Paulo and encouraged enslaved men and women to flee the plantations for urban centers, where fellow abolitionists would provide them with resources and support. Thousands of enslaved people deserted "the plantations in 1887 and 1888 in a massive, non-violent exodus which neither plantation owners nor the state proved able to stop" (Andrews 1992: 151). The full emancipation of people enslaved in Brazil came on May 13, 1888, when Princess Isabel signed the Lei Áurea (Golden Law).[4] In the last country to abolish slavery in the Americas, "emancipation was precipitated not by the masters, but by the slaves" (151).[5]

After abolition in 1888, many former enslaved people migrated to the cities looking for work. Yet, employment discrimination prevented them from taking full advantage of labor market opportunities (Andrews 1991). In response to this discrimination, Afro-Brazilians formed social and recreational clubs to organize leisure and political activities among themselves. In 1930 a group in São Paulo established the Frente Negra Brasileira (FNB, Black Brazilian

Front) for greater political involvement and as a vehicle to put forth Black political candidates. None of their candidates succeeded at winning an election due to the stipulations that made literacy a requirement for voting, the fact that the majority of Afro-Brazilians still lived in the countryside, and internal disputes in the organization (Andrews 1992: 158). The FNB remains an example of Afro-Brazilian political organizing for electoral representation and social support.

The Black press developed alongside these civic and political organizations to enable communication amongst the membership and with the wider public. The Black press includes newspapers and newsletters produced by and for Black people in São Paulo, Rio de Janeiro, and other cities from about 1833 until the 1950s (Butler 1998; Seigel 2009; Pinto 2010). In these newspapers, writers debated the conditions of racial inequality in the country, drew attention to Afro-Brazilian history, denounced racism, and called for particular actions among Afro-Brazilians (Butler 1998).

Photography played a critical role in the Black press. Micol Seigel writes: "Throughout the Black press's pages, sober young men in suits gazed unflinchingly into the camera. Author photos, group shots, regular 'photo album' features and occasional portraits of great men of color (sometimes alongside great white friends, all men save Princess Isabel) made the pages a collage of respectable Black masculinity" (2009: 185). These photographs in the Black press allowed Afro-Brazilian men a means of self-presentation that negated the assumption of inferiority they encountered in everyday life.

The Teatro Experimental do Negro (TEN, Black Experimental Theater) constituted another historic venue of Afro-Brazilian resistance that relied on the visual presentation of Black people. Abdias do Nascimento founded the TEN in 1944.[6] Nascimento gained inspiration to found the TEN after traveling to Peru in 1941 and seeing a performance of the Eugene O'Neill play *The Emperor Jones*, in which a white actor in blackface played the lead. This performance made him reflect on the conditions of racial representation in Brazilian theater, in which "Black characters were either played by whites in blackface or were changed to whites" (O. Fernandez 1977: 7–8). The TEN would go on to produce a variety of plays in Rio de Janeiro with all-Black casts, thereby offering opportunities for Black actors to hone their craft and a place for Black playwrights to realize their dramatic visions. Although plagued by censorship, scant financial support, and lack of coverage from the mainstream press, the TEN managed to produce plays well into the 1960s. Its presence also inspired the development of other Black theater groups. By exploring the conditions of white dominance, discrimination, and barriers faced by Afro-Brazilians, the plays attempted to meet the goal expressed by

Nascimento: "to see that the Negro became aware of the objective situation in which he found himself" (O. Fernandez 1977: 8). The Black press and the TEN were important antecedents to contemporary forms of Black self-representation in Brazil.

Black organizing had to weather the political conditions of two authoritarian regimes, which suppressed Black protest. From 1937 to 1945, Getúlio Vargas led an authoritarian government that dismantled any opposition to his leadership. On taking office, the Vargas regime shut down the FNB as well as other political parties. Later, a military dictatorship ruled the Brazilian government from 1964 to 1985, again suppressing dissent and ruling as an authoritarian regime. The dictatorship sought to prevent leftist political control and strengthen the economy. As part of its strategy of control, "the military dictatorship seized on [Gilberto] Freyre, *mestiçagem*, and racial democracy as tools of a repressive state, closing all discussions and negotiation, and suppressing race-based organizing" (Eakin 2017: 239). They attempted to consolidate their power by exiling and disappearing dissidents and suppressing protest. For example, among those exiled was Nascimento for his outspoken organizing around racial politics. They also censored media and other cultural productions in their attempts to suppress discussions of race and articulations of Black politics. The censors cut out a speech advocating Black power from the film *América do Sexo* (The America of Sex, 1970). In 1975, they banned the television broadcast of *Awakening from a Dream*, a documentary about Carolina Maria de Jesus's book, *Quarto de despejo: Diário de uma favelada* (*Child of the Dark*), which details life in the favelas (Stam 1997: 259). Media censorship was partially informed by "a questionnaire distributed by the Federal Police Division of Censorship of Public Diversions as a guideline for censors [which] includes the following questions: "Does [the film] deal with racial problems? With racial discrimination in Brazil? With American Black Power? With problems outside of Brazil that could have a hidden or subliminal connotation in Brazil?" (Stam 1997: 259). The dictatorship contributed to the silencing of articulations of racism and to the organization of a discourse to combat it.

During the military dictatorship, racial politics would appear to take on a more subtle veneer in the form of fashion, style, music, and visual images in, for example, Black soul dances. Aesthetics and the visual elements of Blackness became important conduits of Black expression while the dictatorship outlawed explicit political activity. During the 1970s in São Paulo and Rio de Janeiro, DJs and other entrepreneurs began organizing soul parties using names such as the Chic Show and Soul Grand Prix at clubs and other venues in working-class neighborhoods.[7] These spaces were attended primarily by people of color, and they played soul music from the United States, like James Brown, and Brazilian music made in a soul style.[8] Attendees wore their hair in Afros, danced in soul dance styles, and wore bell-bottom pants and platform shoes. The soul dance attendees visually refashioned themselves to reflect the current style as part of a process of forming and asserting Black identity.

Black soul dances incorporated the visual element of Black films from the United States, like *Wattstax* (1972) and *Shaft* (1971), by projecting them onto a wall without sound. While the secret police who spied on the Black soul parties discounted the importance of these soundless projections, Paulina Alberto asserts that these films nonetheless communicated powerful ideas: "*Wattstax*—with its vibrant shots of almost a hundred thousand Black Americans sporting Afros, dashikis, and distinctive soul and funk styles, and filling the LA Coliseum for a majority Black community event during which Jesse Jackson led the audience (fists held high) in a rousing rendition of his poem 'I am somebody' (its words flashing across the stadium ticker) and the Black National Anthem—communicates an affirmation of Blackness and racial pride for which no soundtrack or political oration would have been necessary" (2009: 15). Despite the dictatorship's attempts to promote images of Brazil as racially harmonious and without racial difference, attendees of the soul dances identified with African American scenes of Black racial pride and imbibed scenes that promoted Black identities. Michael Hanchard writes that "scenes of Black people crying while viewing the slides and U.S. movies like *Wattstax*, and relating the imagery to their own experience, were not uncommon in the clubs and dance halls where the Soul Grand Prix produced events" (1994: 113). Resistance to racism and the valuation of Black identities took the form of manipulating the body through the optics of style as well as by viewing and identifying with visual images of Black pride communicated in U.S. Black films.

As the dictatorship's repression subsided toward the end of the 1970s, Black organizations began to emerge. The Movimento Negro Unificado contra Discriminação Racial (MNUCDR, Unified Black Movement against Racial Discrimination) was founded in the late 1970s to protest and organize against racism. Two racist events catalyzed the movement's founding: the killing of Robson Silveira da Luz by the police on April 28, 1978, and the dismissal of four Black children from the Clube Regatas do Tietê (Tietê Yacht Club) volleyball team on June 18, 1978, in São Paulo (Gonzalez 1985: 127). Black organizers met in São Paulo and Rio de Janeiro, eventually planning a public demonstration for July 7, 1978, at the Viaduto do Chá (Tea Viaduct) near the steps of the Theatro Municipal de São Paulo. At one point during the demonstration, activists passed out copies of an open letter, which everyone then read aloud in unison. The letter read in part, "We are in the street here today in a campaign of denunciation. A campaign against racial discrimination, against police oppression, against unemployment, underemployment, and marginalization. We are in the streets to denounce the devastating conditions of life in the Black community" (Covin 2006: 72). This reading generated high levels of emotion from the activists and the crowd. People made speeches denouncing racism, and more letters of support were read from different cities and other countries. After years of experiencing a military dictatorship, the act of public protest was a serious matter, and the people who attended demonstrated courage and resolve (Gonzalez 1985; Covin 2006). After the protest, activists organized the movement in other cities through meetings and congresses. They developed an organizational structure, a constitution, and took action to combat racial inequality in Brazilian society and to draw attention to the conditions of Black people.

As the Black movement called for the acknowledgment of racism and the increased representation of Black people in Brazilian life, Zózimo Bulbul's films contributed to that demand. Bulbul, an Afro-Brazilian filmmaker, integrated themes related to Black history and culture into his films.[9] Born in Rio de Janeiro in 1937, Bulbul attended the Faculdade de Belas Artes from 1960 to 1962. In 1962 he acted in his first short film, *Pedreiro de São Diogo* (Bricklayer from São Diogo), directed by Leon Hirszman.[10] After a series of acting roles, he gained the opportunity to work as a camera assistant to Nello Melli, which taught him techniques for working behind the camera (N. Carvalho 2012). In 1974 he wrote, directed, and acted in his first short film, *Alma no Olho* (Soul in the eye). The book *Soul on Ice* by Eldridge Cleaver, a Black Panther, inspired the title. In the film, Bulbul uses pantomime to tell the history of the Black diaspora until the 1970s. At the end of the film, the character, dressed in African clothes, breaks the white chain, communicating the message that "definitive liberty only comes with the assumption of Blackness whose symbol is Africa" (N. Carvalho 2005: 85). In 1974 Bulbul directed, with Vera de Figueiredo, *Artesanato do Samba* (The Craft of Samba), which featured the preparations a samba school undertakes leading up to Carnaval.[11] After experiencing censorship from the dictatorship, he left Brazil for the United States and Europe. On returning to Brazil, he continued acting and directing films and became involved with the Black movement. In 1988, on the centennial anniversary of emancipation, he released his documentary film *Abolição* (Abolition). The film explores the history of Afro-Brazilians from abolition to the present day through interviews with scholars, activists, and everyday people. The film presents the overall theme that, for Afro-Brazilians, nothing has changed from abolition to now (N. Carvalho 2005:

89). Bulbul created films that centered themes of Black confinement and liberation in the context of increasing Black movement public resistance.

Those who worked on behalf of Black racial inclusion gained a political opportunity when Fernando Henrique Cardoso was elected president in 1995. As a graduate student in social sciences, Cardoso had studied racial inequality in Brazil and was open to enacting policies that promoted racial equality (Htun 2004). In November of 1995, thirty thousand people organized by the Black movement marched on Brasilia, the national capitol. Movement leaders delivered to President Cardoso a document outlining a program for overcoming racism and racial inequality, which synthesized their demands. They identified "four critical areas of intervention: education, the labor market, infant mortality, and racial violence" and made concrete demands, such as including "survey questions on race/color in all public records" (S. Martins 2004: 797). President Cardoso responded by acknowledging the existence of racial discrimination and establishing the Grupo de Trabalho Interministerial para a Valorização da População Negra (Interministerial Working Group for the Valorization of the Black Population), charged with developing proposals to combat racial inequality. Under Cardoso's leadership, different branches of the government began to implement a quota system to integrate Afro-Brazilians into government jobs.

In 1996, Haroldo Macedo founded *Revista Raça* (Race magazine), Brazil's first national magazine directed toward the Afro-Brazilian population. Afro-Brazilians grace the cover of the magazine every month, and the pages are filled with pictures of Black people—celebrities, models, singers, activists, educators, and others. The title of the magazine carries the magazine's focus, which is to assert the existence and value of those racialized as Black. The magazine contains profiles of celebrities, announcements for and coverage of events around the country, and articles on racism and discrimination, health and beauty, and dating and relationships. It also contains declarations that "negro é lindo" (Black is beautiful) and of "beleza negra" (Black beauty). *Revista Raça*'s commitment to visually representing Afro-Brazilians challenges the hegemonic whiteness displayed on magazine stands throughout the country such that, as Kia Lilly Caldwell notes, "In many ways, the visual representations in *Raça* have a greater impact on the tone and message of the magazine than do the articles and the journalistic content" (2007: 95). So too, the long-standing success of the magazine undermines the assumptions that visual content with Black people will not sell.

Following abolition, Afro-Brazilians began organizing themselves politically, and from this activism developed vehicles of representation, such as the theater and the Black press. Across these various media moments,

Afro-Brazilians represented themselves as respectable and proud of being Black, and represented their history as one of liberation and confinement, and as beautiful. These media enabled Afro-Brazilians to present their own images and ascribe their own meanings to themselves, which broke from hegemonic, national ideals of whiteness and racial democracy promoted by the mainstream media and government. Next I turn to examples where Afro-Brazilians directly called into question the representation of Blackness in the mainstream media through hearings, manifestos, and protests.

Interrogations of Mainstream Media

As the push for Black inclusion continued, media activism took the form of direct calls for social change in the mainstream media. Mauro Porto identifies the development of "media accountability movements" that sought to hold the mainstream media accountable for their representations through the form of protests, lawsuits, media criticism, and monitoring its discourses (2012: 165). The Black women's organization Geledés sued TV Globo for racial discrimination expressed through the dialogue and actions of the character Raul Pelegrini (played by Tarcísio Meira) on the telenovela *Pátria Minha* (My homeland) in a particular episode. The lawsuit was settled by the telenovela including a scene that addresses the racism of the original scene (Porto 2012: 160). Black politicians included visual representation in the mass media as part of their demands for Black racial inclusion. On May 25, 1998, politician Paulo Paim organized the Meios de Comunicação e Diversidade Racial (Means of Communication and Racial Diversity) seminar, held in the Espaço Cultural Zumbi dos Palmares in the Câmara dos Deputados (Chamber of Deputies) in Brasília. The purpose of the seminar is outlined in the transcript of the proceedings:

(1) Evaluate the situation and the provisions from the research conducted and projects in the academic medium;
(2) evaluate and discuss advances in the state legislature and projects in process in the National Congress;
(3) deepen the reflection, from testimonials of actors, models, and workers in advertising, about the obstacles to overcoming cultural stereotypes about Black people. (*Seminário* 1998: 7)

At the seminar, Deputy Paim sponsored Law 4.370/98, which would require the presence of Afro-Brazilians both in front of and behind the camera in television programs, films, and advertisements. During the proceedings, people spoke in favor of or against such a law, in addition to providing information in line with the purpose of the seminar. The seminar included thirteen scheduled speakers in total, including scholars (e.g., professor of media studies Solange Couceiro), professional media workers (e.g., actor Zezé Motta), politicians, university students, and others interested in the issue of racial representation in the Brazilian media. The law was not implemented. This 1998 seminar does, however, demonstrate an attempt to remedy through governmental means the problems surrounding Black representation in the media.

Through oral depositions, the participants contributed to the process of denaturalizing whiteness in media production. Paulo Henrique Souza noted the small numbers of Black students in journalism schools, recounting that he was the only Black student in a class of forty graduates (*Seminário* 1998: 21). He then discussed the small numbers of Black workers at Rede Globo (now TV Globo): "If I am not mistaken, close to ten Black professionals work with the media, enter into national newspapers. This number is very small if we compare it with the large number of professionals of other races, like whites, who enter into the national network" (21). Souza attributed the disproportionately low numbers of Afro-Brazilian media workers to the lack of economic support necessary for entrance into college. As an aside, he also asked, "Where are the Asians, the Indians, who also don't have space?" (21). His testimony names the low numbers of Black and other minoritized workers as prejudice, thus disrupting the normalization of the dominance of whiteness among media workers.

Zezé Motta, a well-known Afro-Brazilian actor, testified regarding the experience of Black actors in film and television. She stated that mainstream media producers considered Black actors to be "bad, tense, hard," which contributed to the invisibility of Black actors in film and television (*Seminário* 1998: 66). To remedy this issue, she helped to found the Centro de Documentação e Informação do Artista Negro (CIDAN, Center for the Documentation and Information of Black Artists), which identified Black actors, provided acting lessons, and pursued opportunities for them to work. Motta linked the perception of Black actors as bad to two conditions: improvement as an actor required practice, which Black actors lacked due to minimal opportunities for roles in mainstream media (*Seminário* 1998: 68); media companies provided and paid for lessons for white actors who needed improvement, while Black actors were not afforded such resources and were labeled as bad (67). Motta rooted the sparse representation of Black actors in industry practices and voiced the conditions that contribute to their low numbers. In so doing, she challenged the apparent naturalness of media images dominated by whiteness by explaining how they are produced through discriminatory practices of labeling and resource distribution that exclude Afro-Brazilians.

Afro-Brazilian media producers directed the energy in the winds of racial change to their field of visual production in the form of public manifestos, which continue the work of denaturalizing the gaze. In 2000, Jeferson De, a film student at the time, launched a manifesto for Black cinema. Part of a cohort of Black filmmakers in São Paulo, De, along with others in the group, saw success when the São Paulo International Short Film Festival accepted their short films in 1998 and 1999. During a scheduled panel session at the Eleventh São Paulo International Short Film Festival in 2000, De went public with "Dogma Feijoada," his manifesto. He chose the term "dogma" to refer the Dogme 95 cinema movement in Denmark, when in 1995 two directors, Lars Von Trier and Thomas Vinterberg, called for a more realist and less commercial cinema aesthetic (N. Carvalho 2018: 5); *feijoada* is the Brazilian national dish of elaborate black beans and rice. The manifesto puts forth seven fundamental requirements for Black cinema production: "(1) The film has to be directed by a Black Brazilian director; (2) the protagonist must be Black; (3) the film's theme has to be related to Black Brazilian culture; (4) the film has to have a workable schedule. Urgent-films; (5) Black (or not) stereotyped characters are prohibited; (6) the script will privilege the common Black Brazilian; (7) super-heroes or bandits will be avoided" (N. Carvalho and Domingues 2018: 4).

In 2001, at the fifth Festival de cinema do Recife (Recife Cinema Festival), Black filmmakers and actors launched the Recife Manifesto. The group of actors and directors included nationally known figures, among them Milton Gonçalves, Antonio Pitanga, Ruth de Souza, Joel Zito Araújo and Zózimo Bulbul. The document "called for the end of the marginalization of Black actors, actresses, presenters and journalists in the audiovisual industry (production companies, publicity agencies and television networks)" (N. Carvalho and Domingues 2018: 6). Part of the manifesto stated: "This manifesto is a denunciation. We express the end of our patience with the persistence in our audiovisual industry (TV, cinema and publicity) of the existing segregation quota that cannot offer more than 10% of the work to Black actors, actresses, presenters, and journalists in its programs, films, and advertising parts" (6). The manifesto went on to call for legal sanctions against television, film, and advertising agencies that continued to exclude Afro-Brazilians from their material. They made the following demands: "1) The end of the segregation to which Black actors, actresses, presenters, and journalists are subjected to in production houses, advertising agencies and television stations; 2) The creation of a fund to encourage multiracial audiovisual productions in Brazil; 3) The enlargement of the labor market for Afro-descendent actresses, actors, technicians, producers, directors and script writers; 4) The creation of a new aesthetic for Brazil that valorizes the ethnic, regional and religious diversity and plurality of the Brazilian population" (N. Carvalho 2005: 98). During the festival, film director Joel Zito Araújo screened his documentary, *A Negação do Brasil* (2000, Denying Brazil). This documentary visualizes the argument of his book by the same name. The book and documentary demonstrate the invisibility of Black people in telenovelas and the stereotypical characters they depict when Afro-Brazilians are included. The activity of the Recife manifesto demonstrated the problems surrounding Black representation in the media and suggested concrete steps to address it. Both Dogma Feijoada and the Recife Manifesto took the demands for changes surrounding racial representation to the public, thus constituting the media as a site of racial struggle. Their demands call into question who directs and stars in film and television, what themes are included, how Blackness is represented, and how Black actors are treated, funded, and find work.

Brazil's involvement with the World Conference against Racism in Durban, South Africa, in 2001 helped to further facilitate state action regarding racial inequality in Brazil, whose most prominent outcome is, perhaps, affirmative action or quota policies in universities (Htun 2004). However, media and representation of Blackness was also included as concerns for the conference. The importance of this conference lay in its ability to make visible a "global ethno-racial field," which Afro-Brazilian activists could engage in order to construct their claims (Paschel 2016: 17). In preparation for participation at the Durban conference, the government invited university professors, Black movement activists, and state officials to solicit input and reach a consensus on their demands and plans to proceed. The December 2000 issue of *Revista Raça* contains an article about a conference in Fortaleza on October 24 and 25, 2000, during which a group of communication professionals and researchers gathered to discuss the problems of Black representation in the mass media and solutions to address it (Carrança 2000). The "New Role for the Communication and Entertainment Industry" conference was organized by the Palmares Foundation, an initiative of the Ministry of Culture, as part of seven thematic meetings to promote discussions of racial inequality and propose ways to address it. The group was tasked with documenting their discussion and presenting it during the upcoming Durban Conference. During the meeting, Graça Ataíde, a researcher from the Universidade Federal de Pernambuco (Federal University of Pernambuco), made a presentation about the representation of Black people in the media since the 1920s. Luiz Antonio Pillar, an assistant director for a telenovela, argued for the importance of training Black people to work in the media. He discussed the issue of telenovela directors' reluctance to cast Afro-Brazilians in subordinate roles to avoid resentment, which then decreased the amount of work for Black actors. Eliane Borges, founder of a website for Black women, noted that Afro-Brazilians had unequal access to computers and the internet. The coverage of this meeting shows that the image of Blackness in the mainstream media and access to the means of media production remained issues to consider in preparation for the international Durban meeting.

The committees were tasked with drafting a report with recommendations for social change. Black Brazilian feminists were critical to the report and the actions in Durban, as they had prior experience with international forums and were familiar with policy language and consensus building (Htun 2004). The final Durban report labeled the slave trade a crime against humanity and called for affirmative action and other policies for victims of racism. Durban was effective for Afro-Brazilian organizing in that it "legitimized the debate on racism at the international level and recognized the need for remedial actions to benefit the victims of discrimination" (Htun 2004: 82). In 2002, PL 650/99 became law, providing for quotas in public and private universities as well as for civil service jobs (S. Martins, Medeiros, and Nascimento 2004: 805). After 2002, quota programs spread throughout state and federal universities, reserving spaces for a combination of students who attended public school, nonwhite students, low-income students, and female students (Valente and Berry 2017). In 2003, Law 10.639 was passed, which mandated the teaching of Afro-Brazilian and African history and culture throughout the educational curriculum.[12] After the Supreme Court upheld affirmative action as constitutional, then-president Dilma Rousseff signed a law on August 12, 2012, reserving 50 percent of the spaces in federal universities for public high school students (Valente and Berry 2017).

Recent policies of affirmative action and Law 10.639 should not be taken lightly or underestimated. In reference to affirmative action policies, Martins, Medeiros, and Nascimento claim that "many a student of race relations in Brazil would have predicted that such developments could never occur" (2004: 787). By demonstrating the existence of racial inequality and demanding racial redress, activists, academics, and politicians have accomplished nothing less than a policy transformation in a society that considered its populace to be racially mixed and thought itself free from racism. The education arena has proven to achieve more gains from Black protest, evidenced by the increased numbers of Afro-Brazilians in colleges and universities, whereas the visual mass media has shown few changes over the years. Afro-Brazilians have included the production and critique of media within their resistance to white dominance by leveraging the power of the press, the theater stage, films produced outside and inside the country, and magazines. They have taken collective action in the form of demonstrations and manifestos to call for the increased visibility of Afro-Brazilians in the mass media behind and in front of the camera in central roles that are free from stereotypes. Contemporary Black media is only one of the most recent expressions in a trajectory of Black media creation and usage by past generations.

This chapter examines Black struggles for inclusion in Brazilian life alongside Black struggles for representation. Marches, protests, and governmental pressure are among the many strategies Afro-Brazilians have used to advance their interest in improving conditions for Black people in Brazil. They have formed their own organizations, such as the FNB, with media and visual culture emerging as key sites of struggle and expression. The current productions of media and visual culture by Afro-Brazilians are not new and are preceded by past projects in which Afro-Brazilians seized the means of representation to create media and visual culture that conferred their own meanings on to Blackness. Media producers channeled Black politics through manifestos, government meetings, and conferences at the local, national, and international level. These actions made their demands public and contributed to denaturalizing the ubiquity of the dominance of whiteness in mainstream images. They contended that these images were not natural, but rooted in exclusionary mechanisms and that rather than appearing normal, these images should raise questions about who is included and how. The importance of these actions lie in their raising consciousness about and diagnosing the problem of the meanings associated with Blackness and who is included in production so that people can take actions to change it.

Although education has been a critical locus of racial equality legislation, movements for Black representation target media and cinema as sites of racial struggle. Lélia Gonzalez defines the objective of the MNUCDR as "the mobilization and organization of the Brazilian Black population in its fight for political, social, economic, and cultural emancipation, which have been blocked by racial prejudice and its practices" (1985: 126). Black cinema and media producers channel the emancipatory objectives of the Black movement by demanding the ability and freedom to tell their own stories and create narratives that relate to their experiences which conditions the shape and trajectory of antiracist visual politics in Brazil. Djamila Ribeiro contends that after denaturalizing the gaze conditioned by racism, the next step is to "create spaces, especially in places that Black people do not usually access" (2019: 36), a feat that the TV da Gente television network attempted to achieve, which I explore in the next chapter.

2

TV da Gente and Controlling the Means of Media Production

The inability to integrate their visions into mainstream media led a group of Afro-Brazilian media producers to create TV da Gente (Our TV), Brazil's first television network with the mission to diversify the racial makeup of Brazilian programming (figure 1). A *Los Angeles Times* article titled "A New Color in Brazil TV" labeled TV da Gente as "a major advance in the fight for increased rights and visibility" for Afro-Brazilians (Chu 2006). In their attempts to seize control over the means of production and distribute different visions of Blackness, TV da Gente is an example of "televisionary activism," which Cymene Howe defines as "a mediated form of social justice messaging that utilizes the pervasive, popular platform of television to create new 'visions' of social transformation to shape and change, in the word of advocates, 'culture'" (2008: 54). In this chapter, access to the means of media production emerges through the issue of ownership of the network and control over programming as central to the creation of new visions. Those who seek to create new visions of Blackness need to have a hand in determining the content and contours of the representations. As a space of relative autonomy, TV da Gente enabled its workers to ascribe their own meanings to Blackness through program production. I argue that these actions to establish their own television network and make decisions about how they would represent Blackness enact antiracist visual politics by asserting the right of Afro-Brazilians to inhabit positions of authority and control over media production.[1] Additionally, their programming conferred new meanings onto Blackness in the form of middle-class professional workers and program hosts who are central to the program's

FIGURE 1. TV da Gente logo

flow.² These images signify Afro-Brazilian professional workers as Black, which challenges the tenants that money whitens.

TV da Gente challenged racial discourses in Brazil that tend to silence discussions of racism or racial inequality while simultaneously deeming racist any initiative meant to promote racial inclusion or racial equality. Perhaps this context informed the strategy used by TV da Gente's creators in associating the network with Blackness. Launching the network on November 20, 2005, the national Dia da Consciência Negra, reflects this strategy. That date links the network to the national and citywide events celebrating a Black historical figure and Black consciousness, which fit with the network's mission of Afro-Brazilian empowerment through visual representation. At the same time, the name TV da Gente does not refer explicitly to race or Blackness, such as the Black Entertainment Television network in the United States. Articles in English-language newspapers translate "TV da Gente" as "Our TV," but this is not a strictly literal translation. "Da Gente" can be translated as "of the people," referring to the common people or nonelite Brazilians. One of the logos (figure 2) reads "TV da Gente: A Cor do Brasil" (Our TV: The color of Brazil). The logo uses the recognizable pattern and order of the blue, green, and yellow colors of the Brazilian flag, and the brown represents the darker populations. This direct reference to color is as close as TV da Gente's branding comes to referencing Blackness itself.

At its launch, TV da Gente received favorable reviews from the international press, such as the *Guardian* and the *LA Times*. Yet in Brazil journalists levied accusations of racism against TV da Gente because of its focus on the Black population. In "Black TV Ignites Ire in Brazil," journalist Flávio

FIGURE 2. TV da Gente logo with the phrase "The Color of Brazil"

Porcella is quoted: "I think it's legitimate that a channel specialize in sports, politics, sex, religion and any other type of segmentation. I don't agree with a channel segmented for race, color, or religion. Therefore, this means racial discrimination for me. . . . If people are equal independent of color, why does a television channel show only people of one color?" Journalist Thiago Jerke sums up the criticism: "If there is a channel only for white people, wouldn't it be racism?" (Brambilla 2006). The charge of monoracialism was inaccurate because Brazilians of European, Japanese, and African descent worked on and were seen on network programs. Yet, the charges of racism against TV da Gente replayed the familiar strategy in Brazil: label any entity or person who raises the issue of race, racial inequality, or racial inclusion as the *source* of racism. The ideals of racial democracy render racial inequality an inappropriate or unnecessary topic of conversation. Those who seek to call attention to the fact of racial inequality, such as TV da Gente, have to contend with the narratives that threaten to delegitimize them. Most producers employed by TV da Gente were Afro-Brazilians, and the content of the programs emphasized Blackness and discourses surrounding Black consciousness and Black recognition within the city and the nation, but the name and logo did not directly reference Blackness. This strategy did not shield the network from vehement critique of racism. In what follows, I examine the process of founding the network, compare workers' experiences in mainstream media to that of TV da Gente, and then analyze their programs.

Founding the Network

José de Paulo Neto, commonly referred to as Netinho, founded the TV da Gente television network to represent the issues and needs of the Black population. He is an Afro-Brazilian celebrity famous for singing *pagode* music, a form of samba, as well as for working as a television host on mainstream Brazilian media. Netinho outlined the impetus behind the network's creation: "the actual TV does not represent the majority of Brazilians. We are trying to help our own people, given that nobody else seems to want to do it. This is where the real fight starts" (Phillips 2005). Netinho envisioned TV da Gente as a form of entrepreneurship that connected profit and capital accumulation with social and political activism by creating and catering to specific demographics who wanted to consume the message of racial empowerment. He believed the network could demonstrate the profitability of addressing the working classes. He recognized that television is a market-based industry and that television producers must attend to the capitalist structures that precede their entry into it. Netinho wanted to work within a hybrid conceptualization of a television market as both political and profitable, believing he could attract viewers through the medium of Black identity construction while generating economic accumulation for the mutual benefit of all parties involved. Founding a network with a racial mission created a space in which workers could control media production. Yet how did the founder establish such a space?

While Brazilians founded TV da Gente, they drew from resources outside of Brazil for starting the network. From the United States and Angola flowed resources in the forms of inspiration, advice, money, and television programs. The currents that brought TV da Gente into being participate within the "mediascapes" that Arjun Appadurai (1996) identifies as conduits for the contemporary informational flows that facilitate connections in the global world. Additionally, this transnational movement of people, ideas, and money between Black constituencies takes part in the racialized flows that constitute the African Diaspora (Gilroy 1993; Patterson and Kelley 2000; Matory 2005; Thomas 2004, 2007; Boyce Davies and M'Bow 2007). To bring TV da Gente into existence, Netinho gathered the "diasporic resources" of money from Angola, inspiration and television programs from the United States, and media producers from Brazil (Brown 1998). Black television networks and other media groups are resources themselves. They comprise critical sites of Black representation shaped by concerns about Black racial identification and images of Blackness within the public sphere.

The Black Entertainment Television (BET) network in the United States served as the inspiration for TV da Gente. Also, the time seemed right, since in 2003 the government of Brazil implemented the Secretaria de Políticas de Promoção da Igualdade Racial (SEPPIR), Special Secretary for Politics and Promotion of Racial Equality), run by Minister Matilde Ribeiro. Media magnate Robert Johnson started BET in January 1980, seeking to address and represent African Americans by producing televisual content that African Americans controlled and starred in, and that spoke to the needs of U.S. Black audiences. BET acquired and broadcast music videos of African American performers and a short lineup of programs it produced. In this way, BET took advantage of the increasing rates of cable television use and filled a void in African American television representation (Smith-Shomade 2008). Netinho saw an opening to establish a Black television network amid the flourishing of racial equality initiatives in the city of São Paulo as well as nationally. Many Brazilians were engaging in debates about the state of racial inequality and the appropriate measures to ensure equality for marginalized populations. Netinho believed that, like BET, TV da Gente could fill a gap in Black visual representation in Brazil.

The steps that TV da Gente took to seek support from parallel networks outside of Brazil suggest how ownership and control of network business can affect the formation of relationships for soliciting and offering material aid in the form of television programs. TV da Gente leadership first attempted to contact Johnson—even though he had rescinded control of BET by selling it to Viacom in 2000 to gain support for TV da Gente. Communications with BET were difficult, not least because of the additional ownership layer. And Johnson's contract with Viacom prohibited him from revealing numbers and strategic data about BET. The difficulty with BET did not deter Netinho, who then contacted Robert Townsend, the president of the Black Family Channel (BFC), which had launched in 1999. Townsend agreed to help the fledgling network by exchanging programming with it. The BFC was indeed a better fit for TV da Gente, since it produced programming for all ages as well as gospel music shows. (Foreshadowing TV da Gente's own demise, the BFC closed in April 2007, never having found its audience or widespread adoption by cable television providers.) TV da Gente dubbed the BFC programs into Portuguese for its Brazilian audience.[3]

Through Netinho's own television program in Brazil, *Dia da Princesa* (Princess for a day), which aired prior to TV da Gente's launch, he formed a relationship with the key investor who in turn provided the necessary capital of one million Brazilian *reais*: the Angolan leadership. In *Dia da Princesa,* a reality television show, Netinho traveled around to various favelas and working-class areas to surprise women with a day of beauty treatments—hair styling, manicures, pedicures, and new clothes. A chauffer-driven limousine brought the women to each location, and the cameras followed them throughout the day. The program ended with a large party for the chosen princess. During an interview with me, Paula Moura, one of TV da Gente's producers, described the impact of Netinho's popularity, which reached from Brazil to Angola: "In Angola, Princess for a Day [*Dia de Princesa*] was a success, so the president of Angola called him [Netinho] to make some programs there with Angolan princesses. . . . [Netinho] disclosed to the president of Angola that he was the only Black person who had a program on television, and that this wasn't just in a country with Blacks being 50% of the population, and that Black people had to have their own television. So the president said that if Netinho could show the viability of his TV network project, he would invest in it." These actions nurtured the relationship with the Angolan government. The plan involved TV da Gente making its programs for Angolan viewing audiences as well as Brazilians; both populations speak Portuguese, and Angola had little chance of producing much television content as it was rebuilding after the civil war. In this way, monetary capital for television production flowed within Angola and to Brazil to address Black audiences within projects of nation building (in Angola) and national inclusion (in Brazil).[4]

That people of African descent in the Americas and Black Africans in Angola would identify with each other's struggles is not simply a given. Ties, connections, and links between different populations in the African Diaspora must be articulated or made known by different protagonists. Similarities in the lack of access to Black self-referential images pointed to the necessity of Black control of media to produce their own images in the United States, Brazil, and Angola. With this knowledge in mind, he sought connections and assistance from Black television networks in the United States and from businessmen in Angola, all with the goal of producing Black television for Black audiences. Judging from this case, the flow of resources between different populations, in this case African Diaspora processes, are sometimes contingent on protagonists to identify the location of the resources and facilitate their movement.

Space of Control

Founding a network and establishing their own space was central to facilitating Afro-Brazilian participation in and control over developing their own visions of Blackness. Netinho assembled a team of predominantly Black media professionals in Brazil—television producers, directors, journalists, and presenters—to create, produce, and host the programs. While ethnically diverse, TV da Gente did have more Afro-Brazilian hosts and producers than other groups, which made it quite anomalous as a media institution in São Paulo.

Netinho personally asked Conceição Lourenço to take control of the network as its executive producer, managing "everything except for the finances," as she told me. She developed the network's vision, generated the ideas for the program formats and content, controlled the casting and network staffing, attended to any conflicts among the staff, and even appeared on one of the programs as an interviewee. Before leading TV da Gente, she was the editor in chief of *Revista Raça*, Brazil's only national magazine produced for an Afro-Brazilian readership. Her extensive experience working in different media and her distinction as the head of a commercial magazine targeted at the Black population made her a strong candidate to lead TV da Gente.

As one of her first acts as executive producer, Conceição asked Oswaldo Faustino to join her at TV da Gente. She had worked with Faustino at *Revista Raça*, where he wrote a monthly column about Afro-Brazilian culture and history. Oswaldo is a veteran of mainstream news journalism, having worked for the major daily *Estado de São Paulo* for over twenty-five years. He also authored books ranging from collections of children's stories to a book of interviews with other successful Afro-Brazilians. Conceição considered Oswaldo's knowledge about racial issues and experience working in the media useful for a television network that sought to represent the Afro-Brazilian population. His primary responsibility was to appear as Tio Bah, a character on the children's program and tell stories for the audience. He also developed questions for the game show, suggested and recruited guests for talk shows, and generally consulted with producers about all program content. Faustino maintained his primary employment as a night reporter for the newspaper throughout his tenure at TV da Gente; he framed his participation as the fulfillment of a dream to tell children's stories and support the recognition of Afro-Brazilians in the mainstream media.

Working in the Mainstream Media

Many at TV da Gente had many years of work in mainstream media. Despite accumulating years of schooling and experience, they had been unable to increase the amount of Black representation in mainstream media content and they were rarely recognized as professional media workers. They also expressed their frustration at their mainstream editors' failure to approve content that included Black people. For example, TV da Gente's executive producer Conceição Lourenço described to me her previous experiences working in mainstream media. We sat side by side on the couch in her living room with my audio recorder in between us as she recounted:

> I graduated twenty-six years ago and worked in various media vehicles. Black people are totally invisible in the editorial staff of newspapers. I was always alone, I was always the only [Black person]. Then you don't have a voice, the head positions are always whites. Blacks don't have lead positions in the media, in the newspapers, in the magazines. Because of this, the magazine covers, principally the beauty covers, are always white women because the head is always white. So it's a fight to survive the editorial staff. But I always do my work in the best manner possible and never stopped suggesting stories where Blacks can enter. This almost never happened, but I always struck against the same key and never had difficulties with my boss. They said that these stories wouldn't work, but no one ever said this looking me in the eye because they didn't want to do these stories, but I never gave up.

Conceição's main body of media experience was in the area of women's magazines. She links the absence of Afro-Brazilians as a critical mass of writers and reporters and in editorial positions with the dominance of whiteness as a standard of beauty on the covers of the magazines. Elaborating on the types of stories she wanted to incorporate into the magazine, she mentioned featuring Black models in the beauty shoots inside the magazine or on the cover. She also wanted to profile Black people in stories for the magazine, such as having a Black doctor discuss common women's health problems. However, her editor never approved these story ideas. As a Black journalist, she was "alone," "the only one," and did "not have a voice." Conceição continued: "Now, when you enter into the labor market it's very difficult. Whites are going to demand a lot from you and you become a little disheartened. I stayed working as a disheartened journalist most of the time. Without telling someone that you are going to interview them, people don't believe that you are the reporter that made a telephone appointment with them. They stand there staring at you." Conceição discussed an experience she had in which an interviewee failed to recognize her as the reporter with whom they had spoken on the phone. When she arrived for the interview, the interviewee stared at her, startled. When recounting this story, Conceição enlarged her eyes and tensed her face, replicating the expression of the interviewee. This look that expressed shock and surprise at her presence communicated to Conceição that the interviewee did not expect a Black journalist. Her work within the mainstream media caused her to become "disheartened" by the resistance from editors and the treatment she faced with interviewees. Conceição illuminates two modes of resistance she encountered when pitching stories: The explanation she would be *told* would invariably, but vaguely, mention their unsuitability, usually because they "don't work"; yet she often also *sensed* the resistance based on nonverbal behavior, feeling that the editor "didn't want to do the stories." This indicated to her a certain prejudice or subjective decision that became the basis for denial. Thus her story ideas were routinely denied by her editor. The legitimacy accorded to her as a trained and experienced journalist was also denied when an interviewee failed to recognize her as a reporter. As a Black journalist, Conceição is in effect illegible in this role of professional media worker. Her disheartened feeling is linked to the racial conditions of inequality manifested in the treatment of both her and her ideas within her work place.

Visibility is a key theme in Conceição's narrative of her work experiences. In similar ways, the social philosopher Frantz Fanon problematizes the visibility of Blacks within the public sphere through his well-known narration, "Look, a Negro," in *The Fact of Blackness* (1967). In this famous passage, Fanon narrates the unfolding of a public spectacle at the expense of his Blackness: "'Look, a Negro!' It was an external stimulus that flicked over me as I passed by. I made a tight smile. 'Look, a Negro!' It was true. It amused me. 'Look, a Negro!' The circle was drawing a bit tighter. I made no secret of my amusement" (1967: 112). Fanon cannot move throughout the world without others, mainly whites, drawing attention to his race, or the race of other Black people. Conceição feels the weight of her Blackness when her editor will not completely deny her ideas, but rather says that they "don't work" without "looking [her] in the eye." She takes an editor's failure to look at her as proof of the editor's insincerity about her story idea's inability to "work"; it is clear to her that the editor simply "didn't want to do the stories." She experiences one denial through her editor's not "looking [her] in the eye," and she experiences another denial at the wrong end of a stare. The politics of visibility takes various forms including peremptory denial and dumbfounded staring.

Some of the practical constraints Black journalists experienced can be linked to their editors' attitudes about race and media coverage. Tania Cantrell Rosas-Moreno found that Brazilian journalists would not talk directly about race, even when she asked them to (2011: 59–60). She also found that "the respondents' journalistic training has had very little impact on their sensitivity to race and class news issues. In fact, their training did not seem to be training at all" (60). Thus, many journalists are not adequately prepared or trained to address issues of racial inequality. Most importantly, this is the case for editors, who decide which stories will be told. Rosas-Moreno writes: "Most of this study's respondents are editors at Brazil's premier national publications. The position of editor delineates at least some power to act. If editors are echoing journalists' reactions to content creation and production, as well as journalists' foundational experiences, then the system seems more rooted than anticipated and more complexly solidified in the current hegemonic states" (61).

If editors yield significant power, their inability to address race and inequality can inform decisions about content inclusion and exclusion. Afro-Brazilian media producers, who desired to diversify the media content, had to navigate these norms of not addressing race in their respective work places. The Afro-Brazilian media workers I interviewed communicated the limitations they encountered when working within these environments. Several themes emerged from their criticisms of their working conditions within the mainstream media: loneliness at being the sole Afro-Brazilian worker, frustration, resistance from their editors, and misrecognition of their professional status by people who worked inside and outside of their media organizations (Carrança and Borges 2004). Oswaldo Faustino stated to me: "So, it's more or less like this: There is a lack of sensitivity, and many times you are side by side and people don't recognize you. The people that are at your side, principally in our case, they don't see you and they don't want to find out about your story. You don't have prominence within the mass media."

In contrast, workers saw TV da Gente as a space with the potential for them to express their ideas. TV da Gente created a variety of programs in their São Paulo studio space in the Casa Verde neighborhood in the northern zone of the city. They later moved to a studio located in downtown São Paulo that was formerly occupied by TV Globo. The network employed a small staff to develop content and programs. Many of the workers told me that they had more duties at TV da Gente than other network television jobs had ever required, but they saw working at TV da Gente as an opportunity to exercise creative and production control.

As well as seeking to produce new racial representations, TV da Gente producers sought to revise, reinterpret, and reimagine the role of Afro-Brazilians in contemporary Brazilian life. In developing a new television network from the ground up, the producers experienced the potential for a relative amount of creative freedom in their ideas for program concepts and themes. Michael, a program host, seemed to value this: "When you are a part of a television network that is in construction it's very interesting because it gives you the opportunity to involve your creative side." Yet, producers' awareness of how other networks and programs depict Afro-Brazilians informed their own ideas of how Black people should be imaged on the network. TV da Gente program producers articulated what W. E. B. Du Bois termed "double consciousness," with their awareness of the dominant images of Blackness and actively refused to reproduce them (1990: 8). As Oswaldo asserted,

> [Mainstream] society needs to have a different vision of Afro-Brazilian society. To understand this Afro-Brazilian society not as whatever thing that was deposited here, and now they have to live with them. Because we're always seen as indolents, as lazy, as drunks, we are good at samba, good at soccer. Before we only served to drink cachaça [a strong cane liquor], dance samba, and play soccer. Our women were the most desirable because they had wide hips and a large chest. So what do we need? What spaces do we want to occupy? *All of them. I want to be in all of the places, with all the opportunities.* (Original emphasis)

In the cavernous lobby of the magazine publisher for which she now worked, I interviewed Ana Alves, a former program producer for TV da Gente. She described the network in the following way: "It was a space that was giving Black people a range of possibilities in the country, to be Black is not just to play soccer and be a pagode samba player, Black people are intellectuals, actors, well informed. So I thought it was great to open this space for Black people on television." TV da Gente's media producers agreed with other Afro-Brazilians I interviewed in arguing that the primary problem in the dominant media is not the visibility or invisibility of Afro-Brazilians, but rather the stereotypical and limiting images of Blackness. TV da Gente's program creators were responding to the limited portrayals of Afro-Brazilians commonly found on Brazilian network television and the absence of Afro-Brazilians within professional roles. Thus, the dominant regime of televisual representation added some constraint around the creative boundaries of their own processes of program invention. Yet, they considered the network a space of possibility for the kinds of input they could have and the types of images they could contribute.

Images of Middle-Class Professional Workers

The show *Questão de Direito* (The Question of Law) offers an example of how TV da Gente programs presented middle-class, Black professionals. While the show did not focus exclusively on Black professionals, the host and guest positions presented opportunities to showcase Afro-Brazilian professional workers. TV da Gente producers created *Questão de Direito* to show people making a difference in their communities. The hour-long program featured several segments in which the host spoke with his guests about their actions and work in social justice (figure 3). He showcased a diversity of Brazilians taking actions directed towards issues they individually found to be important and of social significance. I interviewed João Gilberto, a former producer for the show, in a small conference room at the television studio where he worked. He outlined its objectives: "to give visibility to diversity, problematize the different forms of discrimination, to give visibility to individual initiatives and institutions that raise the problem of discrimination, and give visibility to these social movements that fight against discrimination that don't always have the space to share their ideas, to share their experience on TV." Overall, the program followed the theme of civil rights and invited people fighting against discrimination and for inclusivity of various populations—religious groups, women, disabled people, and other marginalized communities in the city.

The U.S. program *Judge Hatchett* inspired the creation of *Questão de Direito*. Following in the tradition of *The People's Court* and *Judge Judy*, in her show African American former judge Glenda Hatchett settled small cases brought by private citizens, typically granting awards less than $5,000. Netinho invited Dr. Hédio Silva Júnior, a well-known Afro-Brazilian civil rights attorney in São Paulo who runs a nonprofit organization addressing issues of racial equality, to portray the judge. Silva had also run for a political position in the federal government and testified before the national congress in favor of affirmative action policies. He was the first Afro-Brazilian to work as the Secretary of Justice of São Paulo State. He has authored policy material about Brazilian racial equality and has been outspoken in the area of racial politics and justice. Dr. Hédio's public political profile, his background in law, and his involvement with Black racial rights made him the ideal person to host a court show for TV da Gente. However, the format of *Judge Hatchett* could not be replicated in Brazil, as João explained that "in Brazil we would have a lot of difficulty in making a similar program because there is a lot of difficulty recording the judgment in Brazil. The jury, in contrast to the United States's judicial system, only judges crimes against life, like homicide. It's not like there, where they judge civil material. It wouldn't work to have this program, and perhaps we could think of something else that explores the issue of people's rights." National laws and legal codes prevented the direct reproduction of shows produced in other national contexts, requiring that they modify the idea for the show. Rather than solely represent the settling of a grievance through the legal system by a plaintiff and a defendant, TV da Gente chose to develop a show that would educate people about the personal rights the Brazilian legal system guaranteed and showcase other Brazilians advocating for their rights within civil society. Additionally, they aimed to

FIGURE 3. Hédio Silva Júnior hosted *A Questão de Direito* show

promote diversity by inviting people of different faiths and backgrounds as guests onto the show. As one of the producers told me, it was ultimately "more like Jay Leno" than *Judge Hatchett*.

Questão de Direito required a set that centered around conversation. Dr. Hédio would introduce the segments and discuss particular issues with his guests in an office-like set. He sat at a desk to the left of the stage, in front of a computer, with a big flat-screen television hanging on the wall behind him. The backdrop featured a faux window with a picture of an urban landscape that represented the city of São Paulo. From his seat behind the desk, Dr. Hédio would speak directly into the camera to introduce the topics for that day. To interview his guests, he would move to either a table-and-chair setup, or two chairs facing one another.

While the show maintained awareness about racially diverse guests, the needs of the Black population remained prominent. As the host of the program, Dr. Hédio became a reference for the inclusion of Afro-Brazilians on television and controlled of the particular content and flow of the show. João noted that "although in the case of the program we had an emphasis on diversity, we had a very explicit objective in relation to the Black population. Although we intended for the program to dialogue with the general society, the idea of the television was for segmented media and the content; the interviews were done in consideration of the point of view of the Black population.... It was a television show for Blacks, but not just for Blacks, a television program by Blacks for Brazil." João described the balance required of the program producers to include content that represented the racial diversity of Brazilian people but also remained conscious of their intended Black constituency. As an Afro-Brazilian host, Silva articulated the point of view of the Black population by introducing questions and guests related to racial issues and specific concerns of Black Brazilians. For example, he interviewed a police colonel about his role in preventing the police in the street from discriminating against young Black men. But the program was not about discrimination; rather, it focused on diversity and on, as João said, "positive examples and experiences that were successful in confronting racism." The show aimed to present people who were taking actions in their lives to confront and ameliorate any kind of inequality, rather than diagnosing the problem of racism and discrimination.

With a small team of producers, Silva took primary responsibility for the themes and interviews on *Questão de Direito*. He established the issues for discussion and determined who he would invite onto the show. When producing television programs, TV da Gente's aims were to represent Black Brazilians in particular ways, ways that were previously absent on television. In describing who they wanted to include on *Questão de Direito*, João listed the kinds of Black professionals to be interviewed for the show's content.

> We were concerned to first promote people who would be a reference for the Black community: judges, prosecutors, lawyers, Black scientists, intellectuals, social leaders, politicians. The idea was to give visibility to references, icons, symbols of the Brazilian Black community. We wanted to bring directors of public organizations, of universities, of legislative power, of judicial power, of executive state power, of city governments—there were many city leaders who passed through the program. We wanted to bring artists or popular culture producers of the *periferia* [outskirts] who have success in the peripheral neighborhoods but don't have visibility in the greater vehicles of communication.

Questão de Direito invited people from Silva's network of politically active and professional acquaintances to discuss their initiatives and projects within the greater São Paulo city. The show also featured other team members' personal acquaintances and people they read about in the newspaper. Silva's presence on the show provided an example to viewers of a successful lawyer and advocate who spoke out eloquently in support of programs and initiatives that supported the Black community.

One *Questão de Direito* segment was filmed in a new municipal building in the northern zone of the city that increased the number of courtrooms to

FIGURE 4. Afro-Brazilian judge on *A Questão de Direito*

process small claims cases. Through this expansion of public government offices, the city's legal apparatus could process more cases with greater efficiency. The reporter interviewed a lawyer and a receptionist in the building, both of whom stated that they liked the new facilities and that the building was designed to be accessible to ensure that all Brazilians of various physical abilities could take advantage of the services it housed.

The reporter narrated the proceedings of a case over which a Black judge presided: a former restaurant employee was suing the restaurant owner for back wages after termination. Brazilian legal restrictions around filming court cases prevented viewers from hearing the detailed proceedings of the case, but, as the image from the segment shows, the viewer could see the Afro-Brazilian judge in the center of the screen while hearing the reporter's voiceover detailing the case (figure 4). At the end of the hearing, the reporter asked the former employee if justice was served, and he answered affirmatively. The former employee won the case, and his employer was directed to compensate him for lost wages. *Questão de Direito* then interviewed the employer, who said he would pay his former employee when he had the money (figure 5).

This segment presents the judicial system as a legitimate means through which to seek redress for grievances and injustices that people may experience

FIGURE 5. Interview of restaurant owner on *A Questão de Direito*

within the labor and consumer market. By presenting a case with a ruling on the side of the worker, the show frames court proceedings as a process in which the disenfranchised or less powerful could win. The shot of the building and the communication of its geographical location also inform viewers of where to go to file a suit. The Afro-Brazilian judge presiding over the case represented Black Brazilians as professional workers in positions of power and authority within the legal system. He served as an example for other Afro-Brazilian viewers to emulate or as a source to increase their self-esteem. Thus, the segment aimed to empower viewers through Black representation as well as by providing information.

This presentation of Black professionals on a Black television network defied commonsense notions about the relationship between Blackness and middle-class status. The middle-class category in Brazil was historically formed and discursively marked as white. Brian Owensby (2002) chronicles the emergence of the Brazilian middle class in the course of the country's transition from an economy dominated by an agricultural elite supported by slavery to an urban, industrial environment in which the state expanded rapidly. In Brazil, race inflected the already socially and economically stratified population out of which the middle class historically developed, which informed the creation of a predominantly white middle class within many cities. Owensby demonstrates that, within the urban centers of São Paulo and Rio de Janeiro after 1920, the sectors that fueled the development of the middle classes in Brazil included the government, banking, and the import, export, and distribution of consumer goods. An abhorrence of manual labor and a requirement to present a so-called professional appearance (a shirt-and-tie standard) characterized this gendered and raced category of professional middle-class workers who had the potential for upward economic mobility and social advancement. The class line demarcating the middle and lower classes also served as a color line that restricted many Black and Brown people from "jobs in the commercial sector because appearance mattered, and good appearance was something 'people of color could not have,' as one shop keeper noted" (Owensby 2002: 63). The criteria for presenting a good appearance were not only a shirt and tie but light or white skin as well, making it difficult for Afro-Brazilians to ascend the social ladder. The subjective criteria of good appearance or "an unspoken discrimination against those of darker skins" (64) constrained the parameters around who would be accepted for white-collar or office work, allowing white Brazilians to enjoy a monopoly on middle-class employment, salaries, and status within the expanded market of opportunities for nonmanual work.

In addition to historical exclusion from the middle classes, Afro-Brazilians are also ideologically excluded from the category. Anthropologist Marvin Harris conducted a descriptive study of life in Salvador, Bahia. He writes that "Brazilians say 'money whitens,' meaning that the richer a dark man gets, the lighter will be the racial category assigned to him by his friends, relatives, and business associates" (Harris 1964: 59). More than forty years later, Brazilians continue to articulate the common belief that ascendancy in economic status affects a person's racial classification and the type of treatment he or she should be accorded.

This idea that money whitens has both a class-related and a racial component. First, the concept assumes that class position or wealth is foundational to social inclusion and treatment. This logic posits upward economic mobility as the answer to inequality but fails to address how or why a (Black) person occupies a given class status. This emphasis on class ignores the histories of labor and slavery that created the large Black lower class in the first place. Second, this saying posits an inverse relationship between Blackness and economic upward mobility by associating whiteness with higher economic status, thus rendering the term "Black middle class" an oxymoron in Brazil. Whiteness becomes the designation assigned to those in the middle or upper classes according to this popular theory of the relationship between race and class.

The association with whiteness and middle-class identity continues today. In her study of middle-class Afro-Brazilians in Salvador, Bahia, Figueiredo argues that those who comprise the Black middle class are "out of place"

(2010). She focuses primarily on consumption and writes that "middle-class Afro-Brazilians are looked upon with curiosity when they participate in middle-class social activities and with distrust when they try to acquire or enjoy the symbolic and social goods associated with people with high financial means" (53). Figueuredo sees the practice of consumption and shopping as a significant locus of discrimination against the Black middle class. Because whiteness is associated with the ability to acquire goods of a certain price, Black shoppers may experience discrimination when attempting to purchase products that are considered to be out of their financial reach. By privileging images of Black middle-class professionals, TV da Gente media workers drew attention to this category, knowing that it existed because they inhabited this position themselves. Including Black middle-class professionals on a Black television network undermines the idea that economic ascension whitens.

The Host Position

The role of television show host presented another opportunity to position Afro-Brazilians as professional media representatives who wielded control over their own programs. TV da Gente workers drew attention to the television show host as a position in which Black people were absent. Conceição Lourenco discussed with me her goals for the programs:

> Really, the goal was to show Black people, because if Black people see themselves, they will have more pride in themselves. Our greatest problem is self-esteem, this is not the case for you in the United States, but it's our case here. We don't have a Black program host. There are [white television program hosts like] Faustão, Hebe Carmago, Gugu Liberato, Sonia Abrão—and it's not possible that not one Black person is capable of sitting on the sofa and interviewing in front of the camera? Many are capable, many want to do it. So the intention was this, to make similar programs [with Black hosts].

She presented the program host as a position that mainstream television largely excludes Black people from. Thus, she chose to produce similar programs to those already shown, but with Afro-Brazilians in those roles and positions, such as talk show hosts, for example.

All of the programs produced at TV da Gente were structured around a host who moderated the programs by presenting content and interviewing guests. The role of television show host is a locus of control and authority. Indeed, "the first principle of the television talk show is that it is anchored by a host (or team of hosts) who is responsible for the tone and direction, and for guiding and setting limits on the talk that is elicited from guests on the air" (Timberg and Erier 2002: 3). Hosts tend to have a major degree of control over their shows, both on the air and off. They may act as a managing editor, controlling the segment themes and guests who appear. Additionally, the role of host is a place of professional achievement for media workers. By casting Afro-Brazilians as show hosts, TV da Gente reframed Black people as capable and worthy of running their own programs. They presented Black people as professional hosts and delivered what they considered to be positive examples of Black representation.

TV da Gente mounted *Encontro da Gente* (Our meeting), which was modeled after a typical talk show in Brazil, where a host-presenter introduces the theme for the topic of discussion and then interviews a series of guests about that topic. The program was hosted by Adyel Silva, a former Afro-Brazilian model and current singer at the time of her appearances on TV da Gente. The program had a team of people to find the guests for the segments, but Adyel was responsible for generating questions for the guests. She was given the topic for the show, which she then researched thoroughly.

The content of the show was driven by contemporary issues in the national news. The producers and the host read daily newspapers and weekly magazines to remain abreast of the salient topics cycling through the news media. From these issues, they developed the themes and topics for the programs and generated a list of potential people, usually experts on these issues, to come onto the show to discuss them. Adyel spoke with doctors, lawyers, psychologists, and other professionals about various contemporary topics, such as hyperactive children, laws surrounding child custody, and the effects of parents' separation on children. She also spoke with people on various lifestyle topics surrounding hobbies, food, or other leisurely activities. For example, a cheese retailer came on the program to discuss different types of cheeses, their specific characteristics, tastes, qualities, and recipes for each type. Another guest instructed viewers on how to make miniature bonsai trees. This program did not deviate from other programs of its genre on Brazilian television. When choosing the guests, a producer told me, "We tried to get people who were recommended to us. I invited a lawyer, but he could not come on to the show. So we asked if he knew another lawyer that was Black, and we explained that the focus of the channel was for a Black public, and we ended up getting a recommendation from him for another lawyer." The mainstream news media coverage dictated the topics for discussion on the program. When producing the episodes, the staff tried to remain attentive to the racial identity of the experts they invited onto the show. However, the show's guests were not exclusively Afro-Brazilian.

A general convention of women's talk shows is to have the host control the flow and subject matter of the discourse through their questions and their ability to call on specific guests during specific moments to enter the conversation. By casting Adyel Silva, an Afro-Brazilian woman, in this position, they privileged a Black subject position for this dominant and consistent role on the program. Adyel framed her dissatisfaction with the racial narrative of mainstream Brazilian television in ways similar to many of the other TV da Gente workers: "You watch television programs and see a few Black reporters, but you never see a Black person anchoring the program, so the participation is very sad because it reflects how Brazilian society treats us, how the society sees us. I think this is very sad." Adyel Silva's role as television show host countered the problem of the lack of control Afro-Brazilians have within the programmatic structure of narrative television. Thus, her intervention, and that of TV da Gente's other Black show hosts, was to present themselves as in control of production, presentation, and in positions as experts on contemporary issues.

The End of TV da Gente

Fernanda, an employee at TV da Gente, poetically summarized for me the network's demise: "TV da Gente ended because of the lack of money. If the largest television networks can't secure the funding, imagine TV da Gente, which is just starting. It is difficult to make a child walk if you don't give it any food or space. TV da Gente was a child that was born, but it didn't have the structure to be able to walk and secure its own life, the adults didn't let it." TV da Gente eventually stopped program production and relinquished their studio space in São Paulo. Few people were forthcoming to me about the details surrounding the failure to continue the network. Netinho said that the programs are still circulating through another city—Pecajus, in the state of Ceara. However, all of the former TV da Gente employees have moved to other media organizations in the city. When I asked about the difficulties that arose with the network, many of the workers I spoke with identified balancing the finances and raising interest in the broadcasted content as critical areas of concern. Revenue generation and audience attraction are two fundamentally linked issues for the survival of any television network or mass-market-based product. Ultimately, the scarcity of finances proved detrimental to the continuation of the project. The network did not attract commercial sponsors, which seems to be the general consensus surrounding why they discontinued program production.[5] Some of the TV da Gente workers saw increased representation of Afro-Brazilians on television after—and presumably due to—TV da Gente, within the mainstream media landscape in Brazil. A program director noted the presence of more Afro-Brazilians on mainstream networks and also attributed this phenomenon to TV da Gente as a catalyst that called attention to the dearth of Black Brazilians in the media: "SBT has a Black female presenter, TV Culture, Rede Record, everyone, Globo already had some, but after TV da Gente went on the air, more Black reporters and presenters began to appear. Before, it was difficult. TV da Gente entered the television market with attitude. Other networks started to follow our lead, it was a massive thing." While I cannot prove a direct cause and effect relationship between TV da Gente and the increase of Afro-Brazilians on television, it does seem plausible that TV da Gente made a difference within the mediated terrain of Brazilian life by illuminating the issue of Black representation and thereby inviting others to join the network in filling in the void.

The importance of the TV da Gente network lies in the action of Afro-Brazilian media producers to seize control over the means of representation, thus allowing them to determine the network's mission, program types, themes, and guests. Djamila Ribeiro has asserted the importance of creating spaces that facilitate the entrance and involvement of the excluded as part of an antiracist agenda (2019). The case of TV da Gente reveals that the process to create such spaces can involve mobilizing resources from diasporic Black populations in various locations. These spaces may also experience precarity and remain short-lived due both to factors within and to factors beyond the control of the founders and workers. Yet, founding their own network to put forward their vision proved central to creating the conditions for Afro-Brazilian media producers to gain control over media production.

Having a say or control over the decisions of who to represent and how emerges as an important site for the enactment of antiracist visual politics. Afro-Brazilian mainstream media producers lacked control over content creation and did not have power in numbers to achieve a greater voice in their workplaces. Establishing their own space enabled TV da Gente to choose who they hired, which created a critical mass of Black people both in front of and behind the camera. They established the mission of the network around racial diversity and hired Black and non-Black workers committed to its mission. TV da Gente creators chose to feature Afro-Brazilian middle-class professionals as guests on many of their programs. Positioning Afro-Brazilians as hosts of their programs reinforced this focus on Afro-Brazilians as professional workers and authorities of their own shows. The creators, producers, and hosts of the shows drew from their own professional and personal networks to find Black professional guests to fill these slots. Additionally, as hosts they presented themselves as professional models of control and authority. In so doing, they attributed new meanings to Blackness as central to program production and flow.

TV da Gente's strategy of privileging Black professional middle class guests resembles other representations of Blackness included in projects for racial inclusion and equality in the African diaspora. For example, *The Cosby Show* displayed an "insistent recuperation of African American social equality (and competence), especially through the trope of the stable and unified Black middle-class family" (Gray 1995: 80). The foregrounding of a middle-class image of Blackness was intended to advocate for the dignity, equality, and fundamental humanity of Black people in the context of degrading and pernicious images of Blackness that circulated publicly. Yet in Brazil, where racial lines have traditionally been malleable and one's economic status could grant whiteness, middle-class Afro-Brazilians could potentially opt out of Blackness. Workers at TV da Gente knew that Black middle-class professionals existed due to their very own experiences of work and life and from those of their friends and colleagues. In presenting themselves and others as Black middle-class professionals as part of TV da Gente, a network with a mission of Black representation, workers at TV da Gente demonstrated the existence of the category Black middle class and asserted that Afro-Brazilians could inhabit a middle-class role. Centralizing Afro-Brazilian middle-class professionals does not necessarily displace other dominant images, but it can assert the multiplicity of positions that Afro-Brazilians inhabit and unsettle the naturalized link between Blackness and marginality perpetuated by mainstream media. Although founding and establishing a network was important for control over producing new images of Blackness, Afro-Brazilian media and visual culture producers also deploy the camera on a smaller scale to make their own films, videos, and images. These visions are rich sites to examine the ways in which racism can be represented, a topic I turn to in the next chapter.

3

Animating Racism

Irony and Images of Dissent

On the outer wall of a shop in downtown São Paulo, I see a work of graffiti depicting a Saci standing with his hands up as a police officer gestures for him to stop (figure 6). In the city, ubiquitous graffiti art covers bridges, overpasses, walls, tunnels, and other forms of public space.[1] In São Paulo, known as the City of Walls, *grafiteiros* (graffiti artists) adorn with their own images the endless barriers that surround high-rise condo buildings, offices, and houses (Caldeira 2000). Figure 6 shows an encounter between a Saci, a folkloric figure commonly represented as Black or Afro-Brazilian, and a police officer.[2] The representation presents a typical Saci figure with his identifying marks of having only one leg, wearing a red cap, and smoking a pipe. In folklore, this trickster figure engages in everyday pranks that inconvenience his targets. When someone misplaces an item, they might blame Saci for its disappearance. His red hat enables him to disappear and reappear at will. However, it is not typical for a police officer to stop Saci (because he is a mythical figure). By juxtaposing the figures of the Saci and the police officer, the image skillfully brings into relief one of the ironies of Brazilian race relations: if Saci, a nationally beloved Afro-Brazilian prankster, walked in the street he would probably experience the scrutiny, harassment, and violence the police daily mete out to Afro-Brazilians.[3]

Scholars have found that Afro-Brazilians suffer from police violence disproportionately more than white Brazilians. Basing their work on a statistical analysis of the Brazilian National Household Survey (PNAD), Charles Mitchell and James Wood show that Afro-Brazilians suffer far higher rates of police brutality than their white counterparts (1999: 1015). The magnitude of the problem of anti-Black police violence is also demonstrated through "the

FIGURE 6. Graffiti of encounter between Saci and a police officer. Thiago Vaz.

likelihood that a Black young person be killed in Brazil is 3.7 times greater than that of a white person" (Alves and Vargas 2017: 258).[4] Mitchell and Wood argue that the prevalence of skin color prejudice and the low social class of the majority of Afro-Brazilians make them particularly vulnerable to police assaults and violence. Anthropologist João Costa Vargas describes police assault as state-sanctioned violence against Afro-Brazilians that makes up part of an "anti-Black genocide continuum" (2008: 10). Afro-Brazilian scholars and activists locate police violence in colonial policies developed to control the Black population and as central to the Brazilian national project (Silva dos Santos and Nascimento-Mandigo 2020). As such, this graffiti presents a powerful indictment of racism and Brazilian national symbolism through the visual depiction of the encounter between the two figures.

This public graffiti art suggests the political potential of popular culture—including videos and illustrations—to critique racism in contemporary Brazil. In this chapter I examine Thiago Vaz's Saci Urbano (Urban Saci) graffiti, the *Tá Bom Pra Você?* (Is that OK with you?) YouTube series, and the cartoons of Mauricio Pestana, focusing on the use of irony and parody as key strategies to illuminate various manifestations of racism, including police violence. These representations strategically depict the specific forms that racism takes in Brazil by illustrating scenarios of racism, as they represent the structural, institutional, and everyday moments of racism that inflect the lives of many Afro-Brazilians. In so doing, they critique the many Brazilians who typically consider their country to be racially harmonious or, as Michael Hanchard calls it, "racially exceptional"—that is, more racially harmonious than polities such as South Africa or the United States (1994: 56).

Visualizing the lives of Black Brazilians must include an accounting of their experiences of racism, exclusion, and marginalization. I argue that the visual culture in this chapter foments antiracist visual politics in their break from mechanisms that perpetuate racism, including the national appropriation of Black culture, racial humor that makes Blackness an object of ridicule, and the denial or indifference to racism. The image creators in this chapter deploy irony as, "not just a figure of speech, but a questioning attitude and a critical stance" (J. Fernandez and Huber 2001: 1). In Brazil, irony, parody, and humor are used during Carnaval and as forms of discursive resistance through the everyday observations and sayings of marginalized domestic workers (Goldstein 2003). This chapter analyzes irony as a visual act of communication, which can achieve its effect by depicting a fundamental contradiction within the social order. By acting out and representing acts of racism that deviate from commonsense understandings, Afro-Brazilian visual culture producers animate the contradiction between the general downplaying of racism and the differential treatment they endure as Black people. By representing their experiences to ironic effect, the visual culture presented here confers new meanings onto Blackness and the role of racism in structuring everyday life and experience.[5]

There is a general "incapacity and/or refusal to recognize Black suffering as structural and ongoing" (Alves and Vargas 2017: 264). For example, Nancy Scheper-Hughes notes that it is "'impolite' for the powerful and educated classes to comment in public on racial differences. . . . But this same 'polite' society can thereby fail to see, fail to recognize, that police persecution is now aimed at a specific segment and shade of the shantytown population" (1993: 225). Given Brazilians' failure to recognize or see racial discrimination, enlisting the visual as a mode of racial critique is particularly powerful. This chapter explores images that display "visual irony," what Biljana Scott refers to as images that contain an "ideological component, which sets two orders of reality and associated belief systems into conflict with each other" (2004: 35). The media in this chapter make explicit the disconnect between the hegemonic view of race relations through the lens of racial democracy and the everyday experiences of racism that many Afro-Brazilians encounter. Irony works through the juxtaposition of acts of racism with the symbolism of racial democracy, which has a destabilizing effect on racial democracy's capacity to maintain itself in the face of blatant racism. I locate a contestatory impulse within critical forms of Afro-Brazilian popular culture that explicitly calls into question the durability of the racial democracy thesis by animating the contradictions and ironies generated by the racial order, thus rendering the denial of racism absurd.

Saci Urbano

The image of the police and the Saci in figure 6 is one depiction among many that constitute Thiago Vaz's Saci Urbano graffiti series. Vaz depicts Saci in various situations around the city of São Paulo, on walls, bus stops, park benches, and buses.[6] He takes into account his urban location and audience when selecting his canvas:

> I only depict Urban Saci in the built urban environment. I like this space of the street because it reaches everyone that is public. The newspaper, you have to buy the newspaper. When you have to buy the newspaper you have a culture of readership. Many people do not have a readership culture [*cultura de leitura*] and aren't interested in the newspaper. But in the street, going by bus, on foot, in a car, you are looking around. So it's something very direct isn't it? So I think it [the street] has a very broad canvas for the people. (Rubio 2010)

Vaz notes the democratic potential of representing his art in the street and his use of the visual. He also chooses spaces that align with Saci's characteristics, which he has described as "nontypical," such as on walls around the city. The unexpected nature of such placements suits the legend that Saci can appear and disappear at will.

Vaz describes his decision to feature Saci in a graffiti series in a video interview: "I asked myself, where is Saci? I didn't see him in magazines, in books, on television, nothing. Where is he? On the internet I found him. I thought ah! Let me bring back this popular folklore thing. I was looking for graffiti that referenced Brazilian culture and Black culture [*cultura Afro*] also. Saci represented all of this" (Rubio 2010). He goes on to say that Saci is Brazil's answer to Superman or Spiderman. Saci represents Black culture and Brazilian culture. In addition to the confrontation with a policeman depicted in figure 6, Vaz depicts Saci overpowering U.S. superheroes such as Captain America or Superman, thus endowing Saci with power and authority.

The origin of Saci lies in the stories of Brazilian people, and Monteiro Lobato popularized the persona (Dietrich 2010). "In 1917, staff members of the newspaper *A Folha de São Paulo* began the project that was to become the book *O Sacy-Pererê: Resultado de um inquérito*, conducting a series of interviews on the folkloric figure with readers who responded to an announcement in the newspaper. In recording people's accounts, the anonymous authors depict Saci Pererê as one of the most original and unique Brazilian examples of an international tradition of fantastic characters, created by the storytelling tradition of *o povo* [the people] of Brazil" (146). One of the project's authors, Monteiro Lobato, became a popular author of children's literature, in which Saci Pererê played a role as a central character.

Vaz represents Saci's heritage as Black, enslaved, and poor. He has referred to the figure as "a symbol that represents Black people [*o negro*] in Brazil" as well as "someone [who] manages to live in the middle of the difficulties of the city" (Rubio 2010). Vaz's narration of Saci deviates from other mainstream renditions of Saci, which do not address the slave heritage intrinsic to Brazilian history. For example, an installation called "Legends in the Street" in July 2013 on São Paulo's main thoroughfare, Avenida Paulista, describes Saci as follows (figure 7): "There are days when nothing goes right. The alarm does not ring, a sock is missing and the milk is sour. You're late and do not find the keys. Your dog wakes up weird, tail down. Watch out, he may be having fun at your expense. He, the bad thing, the master of small evils. Always hidden, ready to prank someone. Born in the heart of the forest but learned to travel in a whirlpool and now walks everywhere. Also, he was seen wandering around town here." The plaque does not mention that Saci is Black, nor does it mention that he was enslaved. There have been explanations for Saci's missing leg that do not feature slavery; renditions such as the one on the plaque are not particularly inauthentic. A popular children's comic series by Ziraldo that features the character located the origins of Saci's single leg to his birth (Dietrich 2010). Vaz narrates the story of Saci with decidedly different emphases: "Saci was the son of a slave who lost his leg. He wanted to take off his leg to live freely because he was imprisoned by the shackles. And he lived alone in the forest. He had freedom. And the Portuguese added the red hat to symbolize that he is no longer a slave. He got the pipe from an Indian" (Rubio 2010). Vaz's choice to emphasize slavery, violence, and freedom suggests his particular aim in his project. Vaz's display of a tear in Saci's pants indicates the violent loss of his leg. Brazilian narratives of slavery typically omit violence, just as commonsense notions of race relations in the country today obscure experiences of violence (Araujo 2012; Cicalo 2013).[7] Through Saci's ripped pant leg, Vaz's imagery makes this violent history visually manifest. Vaz depicts Saci as more than a folkloric figure or a cartoon character who happens to be Black. For Vaz, Saci's Blackness connects him

FIGURE 7. Legends in the Street exhibit

with a history of slavery and marks him as a descendent of enslaved people. This history also relates to the circumstances of difficulty in which Saci lives, which is common to many contemporary Afro-Brazilians as well.

Vaz depicts Saci as someone on the margins of society, and those margins are informed by race and racial inequality. The image of Saci and the police officer shows Saci enduring the systematic racism contemporary Afro-Brazilians face at the hands of the police. Another graffiti image shows Saci pushing a cart loaded with a skyscraper and bearing a "recycling" sign (figure 8). The figure resembles the *catadores*, or trash pickers—the men and women who collect recyclables to sell. These men and women scour the cities dumpsters for paper, metal, and bottles, which they pile high on their handcarts and push through the city streets to recycling centers at the end of the day.

FIGURE 8. Saci as a trash picker. Thiago Vaz.

The graffiti shows Saci pushing in his cart the Banespa Building (the Altino Arantes Building), an iconic high-rise in the city. São Paulo is known for its skyscrapers, and the skyscraper in Saci's cart aptly references the city's reliance on *catadores*. The image suggests Saci might well be a *catadore* pushing a cart if he were real, suggesting the racialized contours of economic inequality.

The use of the Saci within images of resistance runs the risk of appealing to the national sentiment that this figure generally engenders. Dynamics of race and racial democracy in Brazil have produced a discursive minefield that renders some Afro-Brazilian cultural forms less resistant than others. Peter Fry (1977) and Michael Hanchard (1994) point to the Brazilian national appropriation of Afro-Brazilian expressive culture, arguing that such processes have evacuated Black culture of its potential for resistance.[8] Yet, the proliferation of Black culture in Brazilian nationalism can also underwrite the very violence enacted against Black people. Christen Smith argues that in Bahia (and I would argue in the south of the country as well), the centrality of Black culture and police violence are two sides of the same coin: "although society continues to hold on religiously to the ideology of racial democracy and to discursively celebrate the vitality of Blackness, the state engages in a racialized necropolitics that, in tension with biopolitical practices, marks the Black body as violable and expendable yet necessary to the maintenance of the nation's saleable world image" (Smith 2016: 7). The Saci figure in Thiago Vaz's series embodies this contradiction in that his status as a Black folkloric character makes him central to Brazilian culture, but his position as a Black character figures him as expendable and thus subject to police violence and racialized suffering.

Arguments such as Fry's and Hanchard's suggest that to represent Saci is potentially to support hegemonic beliefs in racial democracy based on the national affection that Saci invokes. However, images such as the mural depicting his arrest by a police officer transform his nationally celebrated Blackness into a marker of criminalization and deviance. Saci becomes just another Afro-Brazilian man on the street, whose pranks may provoke police scrutiny rather than national love. The illustration of police violence perpetrated against a symbol of national sentiment produces a critique of the racial contours of police violence and enlists Saci within an act of visual resistance rather than national glorification.

Vaz's Saci Urbano graffiti not only offers a general critique of racial democracy and the racism of police violence, but it also addresses the viewer through mockery. The image mocks or chastises the viewer who believes that racism does not exist and who tacitly participates in the Saci mythology. The depiction of Saci under arrest renders absurd the assertion that racism does not exist in the face of such intractable social problems. Viewers, literally and figuratively, stand complicit in perpetuating the racial status quo through their very witnessing of the police scrutiny depicted in the mural, just as their affection for Saci denies that racism exists. The mural makes the viewers complicit witnesses to the enforcement of the racial order and thus participants in its perpetuation.

The image of Saci immediately calls on national sentiment and references the central place of Afro-Brazilian culture within it. Vaz's images implicitly ask how the Black figure of the Saci can be central to Brazilian national folklore while Afro-Brazilian people confront police violence and aspects of racial inequality. It lays bare the two oppositional and contradictory logics of Afro-Brazilian cultural appropriation and anti-Black racism. This irony works through juxtaposed acts of racism with the symbolism of racial democracy, thus destabilizing racial democracy's capacity to maintain itself in the face of blatant racism. The Saci graffiti series achieves its most powerful trickery by using Brazilians' national affection for a Black figure against them, by asking how they can love the representation of Blackness but not living Black people.

Tá Bom Pra Você?

As I note in the introduction, *Tá Bom Pra Você?* is a series of videos that Érico Brás, his wife Kenia Dias, and their two children record and post on their YouTube channel.[9] The videos are comical critiques of the racial dynamics of everyday life, of the whiteness of visual culture in Brazil, and of family life more generally. The Saci graffiti series indicts racism by invoking the inconsistency between the cultural centrality of Black people and the conditions of poverty and police brutality that plague Afro-Brazilian communities. The *Tá Bom Pra Você?* series employs irony to critique the racial order by enacting experiences of racism in order to ridicule the belief that racism does not exist. Additionally, they use parody, "a device whereby an author mimics the style of another literary work, exaggerating it in order to mock the stylistic habits of a targeted author or school of theory" (Twark 2007: 21). The *Tá Bom Pra Você?* series uses parody in their replication of commercials in order to mock the dominance of white actors in them.

After accompanying them in filming an episode of their series in July 2013, I went to their condo to conduct an interview. They ushered me to the patio, where they had already positioned a chair next to a loveseat. As Kenia gestured for me to take the chair, Érico arranged the camera to film us. Sitting side by side on the loveseat, they shared with me information about their backgrounds and their thoughts on the show. Érico Bras works in mainstream media. He had a regular supporting role in the *Tapas e Beijos* (2011–15; Slaps and kisses) sitcom on the TV Globo channel. The sitcom has received several television awards. He was also starring in a musical in Rio de Janeiro. Their YouTube series is a side family project that produces more critical representations of Afro-Brazilians through alternative media. Érico came to Rio de Janeiro from Salvador, Bahia. Kenia was born and raised in Rio de Janeiro. Both Érico and Kenia describe their involvement with Black performance troupes as formative of their racial consciousness. Érico asserted that his involvement with the Afro-Brazilian performance group Ilê Aiyê, which works around instilling Black pride in its members, influenced his perspectives. Before working on his first television sitcom, Érico Bras worked with Bando de Teatro Oludum, another Black theater and music company in Salvador. Kenia worked for the NGO Afroreggae, a Black musical group and community organization in Rio de Janeiro (Ohmer 2016). Érico and

Kenia provided their children a middle-class lifestyle that neither of their upbringings would have predicted.

When describing the point of view they communicate in their episodes, Érico frames the video project as addressing racial democracy and concomitantly denying or downplaying racism specifically: "The idea is to spark the debate. Talk about the false racial democracy that exists in Brazil. That's why we end each episode by asking if it's OK for those who watch it. If so, say why. If not, also talk" (M. Azevedo 2013). By depicting everyday acts of racism, the videos illuminate the false nature of racial democracy. The couple brings this racial critique to bear on their reading of everyday social relations, which the *Tá Bom Pra Você?* videos articulate.

The show's name requires explanation. The idea and name of the show emerged from family discussions and their daily observations. Their daughter "wanted to know why subjects about Blackness, which are discussed at home, are also not carried out at school. So we decided to create the channel to show the other side of the coin" (M. Azevedo 2013). Already having knowledge of racial inequality, while watching television her daughter noticed that she felt excluded from programs and commercials that featured predominately white casts. They stumbled on the name when thinking it was not good or OK to have an absence of Black people on television. The phrase "is that OK with you?" also has significance in Brazilian everyday conversation; it is commonly asked to inquire if everything is satisfactory and requires a response from the person asked. The response given is usually agreeable or affirmative. Rarely would someone say that it is *not* OK. The episodes typically depict a racist practice or raise the issue of racism and then end with the family asking, "tá bom para você?" directly to the camera, addressing the viewer. Here the question could be asking, "Do you agree with this?" or "Is that OK with you?" or "Is this good for you?" As many Brazilians would verbally disagree with racism, the question would generally elicit the answer "no," which goes against the affirmation that the question typically elicits. Combining a question normally used innocuously in everyday situations with the serious issue of racism reverses the tone of the question from one of innocent inquiry to a more challenging stance. The family visualizes this tone in the pose with which they end the episodes, with the four of them looking intensely into the camera and frowning. Finally, ending the videos that depict racism with a question that requires a response resists the general tendency to avoid discussions of racism by obliging the viewer to engage with the material that the videos presented.

One video titled "Pedrada" critiques racism by depicting the occurrence of a middle-class Afro-Brazilian being mistaken for a maid or service worker in

FIGURE 9. The "Pedrada" sketch from *Tá Bom Pra Você?*

her own apartment.[10] Érico plays a mason coming to the family's apartment to fix something. He knocks on the door. When the house's owner, Kenia, answers it in a bathrobe with a towel around her head, the mason assumes she is the maid. When his repeated question, "Is the owner of the house here?" does not produce a more suitable substitute, he proceeds to address her as the maid. He says, "When the cat's away the mouse will play," indicating that the maid is taking advantage of her boss's absence by dressing in casual clothing and delaying her work. In a scene that Érico renders humorous with his facial expressions, the mason proceeds to flirt with Kenia, still convinced that she is the maid (figure 9). Finally, Érico (in a dual role accomplished by simple camera work) returns home with the children, and the mason realizes his mistake. He openly expresses his surprise that Kenia is the homeowner. The video ends with the family assembled as Kenia asks, "Is that OK with you?"

Using Patricia Hill Collins's (1992) idea of "controlling images," Caldwell claims that "controlling images of Afro-Brazilian women as domestics, sexual objects, and social subordinates influence common sense understandings of their proper place within Brazilian society" (2007: 69).[11] The video depicts just how controlling this image of Black women as maids can be, when Kenia cannot be recognized as the homeowner. Representing these interactions also critiques this stereotype in a humorous way. At the end of the video, the mason realizes his mistake and is forced to see Kenia in a new way—not as a maid but as the condo's rightful owner. Érico opens his eyes wide to register his surprise at this realization, which adds humor to the encounter. Kenia's final question, "Is that OK with you?" has multiple meanings and audiences. She might address the mason, who is off-screen (as he must be, since Érico plays him as well as Kenia's husband) at the conclusion of the video, as well as the viewer. Of the mason she may be asking, "Is it OK with you that I own my home?"—or it might be, "Is it OK with you that your assumptions are racist?" Of the viewer, she might be asking if they are comfortable with a society in which Kenia will be mistaken for a maid because of her race, or conversely whether it is OK for a Black family to own a middle-class home like hers.

Many of the videos in the series act out quotidian moments of racism, discrimination, or everyday micro-aggressions that Afro-Brazilians encounter in their everyday life. Kenia notes that "everything serves as an element of creation. We bring our personal experiences to the videos" (M. Azevedo 2013). The family also asks viewers to contribute their own stories of racial discrimination for consideration for future video dramatization. This impulse to act out real-life scenarios with exactness implies a kind of irony. The videos demonstrate what racial dynamics look like in a context in which people either deny or downplay the existence of racism. Their videos bring into relief the ideas both that Brazil is a racial democracy with cordial race relations and that racial difference inflects social encounters. By showing racially inflected social relations, the videos take on a pedagogical quality, reflecting Black experiences for viewers who might share them, as well as those who would not.

The family also makes parodies of commercials on Brazilian television. Television advertisements on mainstream television rarely include Afro-Brazilians, a point the videos point out through a "Margarina Black" (Black margarine) commercial. All four members of the household sit on the parents' bed (figure 10). The children eat bread and margarine as their loving parents look on, enacting a scene of ideal domestic life. The voiceover states: "You know that day when you wake up happy. Together with your family. Your spouse's dream has come true. Your daughter got an A in school. Your son passed the *vestibular* [the college entrance exam]. And you were promoted. Black Margarine—because Black people also eat bread. Black Margarine—

FIGURE 10. "Margarina Negra" commercial from *Tá Bom Pra Você?*

because every family deserves to be happy." The commercial ends with the family hugging one another to express their happiness and love.

The choice of margarine has particular significance in Brazilian advertising. In the parlance of advertising agencies, "margarine families" are families that project an idealized image of family life in commercials, and they are mainly depicted as white. By re-creating these commercial scenes with themselves as the actors, the family's videos call attention to the exclusion of Black people from this idealized image. The "Margarina Black" commercial parodies commonsense assumptions about the representation of ideal families, race, and social class, disturbing the presumption of whiteness as an idealized image. In so doing, their commercial interrupts and reconfigures key images of family life in Brazilian commercial television.

Yet sincerity complements parody and satire here. The other reason the video features margarine is, as Érico says, "Black people who live in favelas consume margarine, toilet paper, cookies, milk" ("Érico Brás" 2018). Érico positions himself and his family as the legitimate advertisers of such a product. In the video, the only mention of race is in the product name, Margarina Black. The family insert themselves into the commercial space as literally as they can. The main distinction between the video and the commercials it parodies is the race of the participants. Érico observed in an interview that "obviously there is racism on TV. In advertising then! Do only non-Black people have the dignity to sell products?" (ibid.). The family came up with the idea for the commercials after constantly hearing that Black people cannot sell a product (*o negro não vende*). This implies that either Afro-Brazilians do not have the money to buy the product being advertised or that Afro-Brazilians in commercials do not present the standard image of aspiration. This logic keeps Black people from acting in commercials. So the "Margarina Black" skit hovers somewhat ambiguously between parody and sincerity in its attempts to forge an image of Afro-Brazilian inclusion in visual culture.

Érico and Kenia's YouTube videos have attracted anywhere from 8,000 views to 16,000 views, as well as comments from viewers. The majority of the comments on Érico and Kenia's videos are positive. Many express laughter by writing "Hahaha" or "*rsrs*," which is laughter written in Portuguese. A commenter named David Avelina paid tribute to the series' underlying intent: "Great videos! In a society where in the general media Black people are the exception, here come other videos. Open your minds people, the industry is Cruel!"

Some people who commented recognized their own experiences in the scenarios. In response to the mason video, Tatiana Gomez wrote, "I have already lived this in my skin [*vivi na pele*] other times." In the introduction I describe the team filming a video drawing attention to the stereotype of Black criminality, which they titled "Atitude Suspeita" (Suspicious attitude). In that video, the daughter plays a white woman who fears that two Black men on the street will harm her. In fact they are undercover cops who then arrest her for racism. About "Atitude Suspeita," commenter Valdemeir Viera wrote (in all capital letters): "This story was the truth. Anyone who hides their cellular phone or bag when they pass a Black person should be addressed and sued for racial discrimination." Roberto Black also wrote in all capitals about the video, "very good, this happens a lot." Hud Black Power commented, "Haha . . . excellent video, it draws in a funny form the reality of many Blacks."

The parodies of commercials elicit comments affirming that Black people have the capacity to purchase or create their own products. Carlos Andre Soares dos Santos wrote of the "Margarina Black" commercial, "Great video. It demonstrates that people think that rich Black people don't exist or are rare, but they exist." Commenters mentioned the possibility of boycotting companies and products that refuse to have Black spokespeople. The Reverend José do Carmo da Silva wrote, "Get the hint and protest. I believe that we have the potential to create our own products and boycott the racist businesses that only put white people in their commercials. In a country that is majority Black and Afro-descendent, if there was mobilization, the thing would break [*se houver mobilização a coisa quebra*]." Two viewers wrote comments requesting a commercial for toothpaste, which Black people rarely appear in, and Érico and Kenia complied with "Total Protection Black," released on

June 9, 2013, which received 7,967 views and 33 comments. Rodrigo Rocha wrote, "YES THIS IS THE TRUTH, let me remind all the publicists that Black people also have white teeth, and besides this consume these products. It would be great if there were Black businesses, made by Black people. I hate using products that don't represent me."

Some comments express confusion. In response to the mason video, one commenter simply wrote, "I don't understand." Beto Guinne responded by writing, "Really? You don't understand? I'll explain to you my dear. This is very common in this racist country where we live that a person knocks on the door to a house or apartment in a middle class building and asks this racist question when the door is answered by a Black person, even when they are not dressed in clothes that identify them as maids. Here comes the catty question: CAN I SPEAK WITH THE OWNER OF THE HOUSE? Understand now?" Another commenter on the "Margarina Black" skit, Jairo Robinho, wrote, "how so? Incredibly, Black people also eat margarine? I don't understand the joke." This commenter was confused by the parody in that he only saw it as showing that Black people eat margarine, which seemed obvious, He did not understand that the commercial was critiquing the lack of Afro-Brazilians in commercials about margarine even though they do consume the product. Another commenter, Marco S., explained to Jairo Robinho, "It's not a joke, it's irony. None of the margarine commercials in Brazil have Black actors." "Atitude Suspeita" encountered more complex resistance when Petro S. wrote, "cool video, but it's ugly to keep bringing up a climate where the woman at the end is racist. . . . people, without clothes and the area they would say that someone is exercising, it's natural that you're afraid when someone is running for nothing in the street independent of the color of one's skin." This comment refuses the racial interpretation of the scenario apparent to so many other viewers.

Tá Bom Pra Você? diverges from the relationship between race and humor found in mainstream media in Brazil and other Latin American countries. Racial humor in Brazil can rely on stereotypes of Black people as a source of humor or for a joke. This humor plays on, popularizes, and naturalizes negative stereotypes of Black people. The general belief that Brazil specifically and Latin America generally are nonracist societies perpetuate the existence and use of racial humor. As Edward Telles points out, "a sense of political correctness, which often acts informally to censor jokes in the United States, is relatively absent in Brazil" (2004: 154). Mainstream television programs that deploy Blackness and humor generally structure jokes at the expense of Black people. The everyday speech of many Brazilians contains jokes about Afro-Brazilians being monkeys or comparing them to animals, which transmits racist stereotypes on a quotidian level. The use of blackface continues in Brazil and in other Latin American countries and is one of the most explicit forms of race, racism, and humor in Latin American mass visual culture (Rivero 2005). Smith recounts a scene from the show *TV Xuxa* on TV Globo that she watched in 2008, which featured an amateur theater group from Curitiba calling itself the Sanitary Napkins.

> The two white-mestiza performers dressed as a couple going to a *forró* [a traditional harvest dance]. One woman was in drag, wearing men's clothing (hat, pants, black suit jacket, and mustache) and no face paint. The other had her face painted pitch black and wore bright red lipstick, a bright red dress, and an exaggerated Black Afro wig with a big red bow. She also wore a long-sleeved black undergarment and stockings that made her arms and legs black as well. The petticoat under her short red dress gave her a child-like and absurd appearance. Taking all of this together, she purposely tried to portray herself as "ugly." As she walked onto the stage, she ironically introduced herself to Xuxa, the program's host, in character, saying, "Tell me I'm not a beautiful *morena*." The two performers proceeded to present a skit in which the man excoriated the "Black woman" as smelly, ugly, unkempt, and disgusting and called her a *porca* (pig). (Smith 2014: 115)

Smith describes the judges' responses to the performance as complimentary. She concludes that "the racialized, gendered, and sexualized implications of this performance went overlooked or at least unremarked" (Smith 2014: 116). Images such as these may produce feelings of shame, embarrassment, or anger for the people they parody.

Racism channeled through humor, or "recreational racism," is a standard feature of mainstream television (Moreira 2019). The *Zorra Total* series, a satirical show that pokes fun at aspects of Brazilian culture, regularly shows the actor Rodrigo Sant'Anna in blackface and drag to play the character Adelaide, an Afro-Brazilian woman. He sports darkened skin, a prosthetic wide nose, a mouthpiece with a gap between the teeth, and a dress in a bright, even lurid color. The oafish character talks with an exaggerated lisp. Activists and commentators have denounced the skit as racism. Smith contends that these racialized performances cannot be separated from the violence perpetuated against Black and brown women's bodies (2014). As Christina Sue and Tanya Golash-Boza say of similar jokes they heard in Peru and Mexico, jokes like these "maintain colour-blind ideology and serve as everyday mechanisms in the maintenance of a racialized social structure" (2013: 1585).

The *Tá Bom Pra Você?* videos that take on stereotypes may offer some pleasure to the viewer who has experienced such forms of racism. I have been identified as a maid and a prostitute and been directed to service elevators during my research visits in Brazil. Not once did I voice my disgust to the perpetrator of the stereotype due primarily to my inability to think fast enough on my feet. The videos in the series resolve the interpellation through stereotype with the perpetrators realizing their mistake in embarrassment. In the mason video, the mason realizes his mistake when confronted with the family and expresses shock when confronted with his own assumptions that Kenia was a maid. In "Atitude Suspeita," the perpetrator of the stereotype is arrested for racism. For the viewer who may have had these experiences, the narratives can offer satisfaction when executors of the racist acts must confront their racist perspective.

Tá Bom Pra Você? turns the object of the joke away from Black people and toward the social system and individuals that refuse to interpret the many forms that racism takes in Brazil. The videos mock Brazilians who deny that racism exists, implicitly asking how the family's experiences with racism can exist if racism does not exist. They expose the absurdity of racial discourses in Brazil that downplay racism through the representation of their own lives. They expand the traditional understandings of racism to include the assumption that Blackness implies lower socioeconomic status or criminality. The series also frames the absence of Afro-Brazilians in commercials and on television in general as a form of racism. For Brazilians who continue to believe that racism does not exist or that only explicit exclusion can be racist, the joke is on them.

Mauricio Pestana

Mauricio Pestana is perhaps best known as the head of the editorial board of *Revista Raça*, Brazil's longest running magazine directed toward the nation's Afro-Brazilian population. He has authored at least twenty-five illustrated books on racism and racial dynamics in Brazil, on historical events in Afro-Brazilian history, and on groups of Afro-Brazilians in various regions of the country. He has produced numerous pamphlets on subjects such as racism in Brazil and an Afro-Brazilian history board game. In keeping with this chapter's focus on explicit critiques of racism in popular culture, this section focuses on Pestana's political cartoons, which poke fun at and expose the racial dynamics of Brazilian life. By clearly representing scenes of racism, these cartoons visualize the ways in which racism operates in Brazil. Pestana's cartoons ultimately have a similar message as the *Tá Bom Pra Você?* videos—to clearly depict racial dynamics—yet he attends more closely to the institutional nature of racism. Institutional racism can be defined as, "a pattern of subordination of Blacks by Whites at the societal level that was the outcome of the interaction of a number of social institutions, such as systems of education, policing, and the labour market" (J. Scott and Marshall 2015). Pestana's cartoons presents the relentlessness of racism in the lives of Afro-Brazilians by depicting the ongoing pattern of racism through police assaults, discrimination in the labor market, and misrepresentation on television.

Pestana started publishing cartoons while he was still in college. He went to work for *Isto É* (This is), a magazine that contested the military dictatorship and state repression. The left-wing politics of many of his colleagues influenced Pestana, but Pestana also circulated within the Black community and among activists of the Black movement. In depicting racism in Brazil, his cartoons contradict the claims that racism didn't exist in Brazil. Pestana was able to find his niche as a political cartoonist, which united his involvement with Black politics and his magazine background. His cartoons typically feature simply drawn figures and scenes in black and white. They depict Afro-Brazilians as pitch Black, and white Brazilians as colorless. Brazilian racial categories have been characterized as fluid; individuals may experience ambiguity around their racial identification. Elizabeth Hordge-Freeman found that "racial socialization is characterized by ambiguity and a de-emphasis on rigid racial and color classification" (2015: 154). In Pestana's cartoons, Brazil's rainbow of color gradations reduces to depict racism and its consequences in two stark tones.

One of his classic cartoons that demonstrates the subtlety and specificity of racism in Brazil is on the cover of his book, *Racista, Eu!? De jeito nenhum!* (2001; Racist, me!? There's no way!). The image depicts the title as a bit of dialogue spoken by a white male Brazilian addressing a Black male Brazilian. Wearing glasses, a suit and tie, appearing to smile, and with his arm around a Black Brazilian, the white Brazilian exclaims, "Racist, me!? There's no way!" The Black man looks the white man directly in the eye with his brows furrowed and his mouth grimacing, seemingly expressing his discontent and disagreement. This cartoon suggests the common denial of racism and the fury of its victims in the face of this denial. It depicts two markedly different perspectives existing side by side and in the bodies of whites and Blacks—one where no racism exists and one where it does.

One of the themes Pestana tackles most frequently is police violence. The very first cartoon in *Manual de Sobrevivência do Negro no Brasil* (1993; Survival manual for Blacks in Brazil) which he coauthored with Arnaldo Xavier, depicts a group of white police officers breaking down the door and invading the home of an Afro-Brazilian man. The police enter the home to find the Afro-Brazilian man inside watching on television a police officer beating a Black man with a billy club. As the police enter, the man exclaims, "wow these scenes from South Africa are so moving that they seem to be happening right here!" (5) His statement comes true as the police beat him too. When Pestana published this cartoon, apartheid was still in place in South Africa. The cartoon calls attention to routine police raids of favela communities for suspected drug or criminal activity in Brazil. By drawing a parallel between South Africa and Brazil, it mocks the belief in Brazilian exceptionalism and posits the two countries as equivalent. The subtext is clear: if the scenes from South African *seem* to be happening right here, that's because they are.

Another image depicts the police shooting an Afro-Brazilian suspect and asking for his documents afterward. A third cartoon represents an Afro-Brazilian man showing his documents to a police officer and telling this police officer, "You are talking to a lawyer" (1993: 7). In the next frame, the policeman arrests the Black lawyer and tells him, "Talk about a lawyer—you'll need one for offending an authority" (7). Another shows two Black men sitting in a favela, one saying, "Pedro was the sixth man killed by the police" and the other answering, "Oh that's why the unemployment rate is going down." These cartoons all communicate that police violence is a problem for all Afro-Brazilians across class levels. The lawyer and the favela residents alike experience abuse of police authority.

In Pestana's *Manual de Sobrevivência do Negro no Brasil*, the cartoons accompany a text that lays out forty-five numbered pieces of advice for Black survival in Brazil. Number three states, "Whenever you see a policeman whether from a very short, medium, or long distance, *don't run*! Not even if it would be to catch the last bus available in the night or take shelter from the rain. *Don't stand*, either. And if possible, *don't move*" (1993: 6). This contradictory advice underscores the dilemma of Afro-Brazilians interrogated by the police: every move they make is the wrong one.

Many of Mauricio Pestana's cartoons take television in Brazil and its hegemonic whiteness to task by placing it in conversation with Afro-Brazilian viewers. In one scene he draws two Black men walking and talking. The one man asks, "Is your television black and white too?" and the other responds, "No it's only got whites." Another cartoon shows a Black man watching television under a bubble showing his apparent thoughts: "Robber, drunkard, vagabond, beggar, slave . . . wow! Is there anything else you would want me to be?" These two cartoons lay out the hegemonic whiteness and stereotypical Blackness that comprise Afro-Brazilian representations on television. Another cartoon shows a Black young woman and her father watching television. The daughter says, "I think I don't want to be an actress anymore, Daddy. If

I have to wash clothes, iron them, serve people, I work like this here!" The statement exposes the narrow range of parts for Black actresses in Brazilian television.

Racism through racial slights, micro-aggressions or explicit racism, usually in the context of employment, is another major theme in Pestana's work. In one cartoon, a Black woman faces a white man seated at a desk, her apparent interviewer. The white man says, "You speak English, right? Oh too bad, we need someone who speaks German," to which the Black woman replies, "I speak German too." He retorts, "Sorry, we don't hire polyglots." The cartoon communicates the message that qualifications can be twisted to ensure that a Black person will be refused work. Another cartoon shows a Black man opening the door to an office, asking, "excuse me, is this where you need an office clerk?" to which the white man seated responds saying, "it was." On seeing that a potential applicant is Black, the manager claims that the position is filled or no longer available. In these cartoons, people are categorized and judged racially, rather than through merit or skill.

Pestana's representations offer Afro-Brazilian perspectives through the enactment of these very experiences. He is a photographer of reality. He takes what he observes and makes a caricature of reality. He takes the very serious topic of racism and renders it through humor by communicating the contradictions within society. Pestana draws from his own observations, perceptions, and lived experiences to depict these scenarios. Some of his readers only recognize that they have experienced racism after seeing their own experiences mirrored in his cartoons.

Pestana does not find humor in experiences of racism. Rather, his cartoons make fun of the Brazilian social context that downplays the existence of racism or outright denies it all together. In Pestana's work, Afro-Brazilians are not the butt of jokes—racism's deniers are. Like the other artists whose work this chapter analyzes, Pestana makes the "commonsense" attitude that racism does not exist the butt of his jokes, asking how the reality he depicts can be consistent with the nonexistence of racism. He takes the experiences of Afro-Brazilians and renders them in visual form for anyone who cares to look.

Afro-Brazilian media producers visualize their experiences with racism exhibited in everyday and institutional contexts, which differs from the limited ways that mainstream media represents racism. The sitcom *Mister Brau* provides an example of how mainstream media represents racism by downplaying it and appealing to ideals of racial democracy.[12] Released in 2015 on TV Globo, *Mister Brau* follows the relationship of Mister Brau (Lázaro

Ramos), a famous singer, and Michele (Taís Araújo), his wife, manager, and backup dancer.[13]

In the second episode of the first season, Mr. Brau decides to invent a multihued Band-Aid after cutting his finger and finding that "flesh-colored" Band-Aids are only made in the color of light skin. However, a U.S. company already makes such a product. When meeting with a representative from the U.S. company, Mr. Brau states he did not want to replicate the U.S. product, but rather, "Our intention, my intention, was to always mix the different colors. Mixing is always more healthy." Through this and other conversations, Mr. Brau undermines understanding racism through a binary model of Black and white. "In place of such a binary model, Mister Brau suggests its opposite—that is, a return to the ideal of a racial democracy within which racial mixing is one of the defining characteristics of Brazil and race is erased as a deciding factor in one's socioeconomic position" (Carter 2018b: 351). Although Brazil has shifted in acknowledging racism, this episode of *Mister Brau* demonstrates the continued hold that ideals of racial democracy have.

These examples of racism on mainstream television are important because they demonstrate the dominant ways in which racism is discussed. Researchers have established that many Brazilians downplay the veracity of racism, fail to recognize the systematic and institutional aspects of racism or racial inequality, and understand racism only as an individual act. Thus many people fail to understand how social and economic inequalities are structured by race. The media projects in this chapter complicate the representation of racism. Saci Urbano, the *Tá Bom Pra Você?* video series, and the cartoons of Mauricio Pestana represent with clarity and exactness the range of experiences of racism that Afro-Brazilians encounter. They depict racism in everyday encounters, such as being mistaken for a maid in one's own home. Érico and Kenia, Thiago Vaz, and Mauricio Pestana point to forms of structural racism in the pattern of police violence enacted against Black people, the routine absence of Black people in the mass media, regular discrimination in the job market, and the assumption of Black people occupying a service position. By depicting racism as they observe and experience it, these artists animate the contradictions in the racial order and employ irony to expose the absurdity of those who choose to ignore or downplay racism. By documenting, representing, and distributing their experiences in visual form, Afro-Brazilian media producers communicate the contradictions, inconsistencies, and tensions of Brazilian racial dynamics.

The images in this chapter made Blackness central, and it takes on new meanings that illuminate the vulnerability and potential of Black people. While Saci is a nationally loved figure, as a Black figure he remains vulnerable to the violence and poverty that structure the lives of many of the country's people whose forebears were enslaved. In the *Tá Bom Pra Você?* videos, Black women have the potential to inhabit the position of maid and/or middle-class homeowner. Black families do have the potential to advertise products and represent ideal visions of domestic life. Yet, racist interpolations of Afro-Brazilian women and families confine them to invisibility and fix them as service workers. In this visual culture, Black people are the central protagonists and viewers follow their struggles and situations. The Brazilian sketch comedy show *O Grande Gonzalez* (from 2015; The great Gonzalez) has gained popularity, and its sketches have attempted to address racism through irony and satire. Yet, Black people have remained absent in these sketches (Carter 2018b). The images and videos in this chapter present uses of humor, irony, and parody that center Black subjects and their perspectives. By deploying the views of Black subjects, the videos and images turn the mirror toward Brazilian people and society. Afro-Brazilians are not the object of ridicule; instead, the presence of racism and the concurrent denial of it are presented as absurd. Grotesqueness lies not within Blackness, but within a system whose celebration of Blackness, harmony, and mixture sustains deeply entrenched forms of racial inequality and violence. The next chapter considers the ways in which films made by Afro-Brazilians render racism in the visual organization of society from the perspective of Black children.

4

Independent Lenses

Learning to See in Afro-Brazilian Film

At the end of June 2013, I attended a launch party in downtown São Paulo for Jefferson Santos's documentary, *A Formação do Olhar* (The formation of looking). Several dozen people stood around the multipurpose room mingling when I arrived, while the filmmaker made his final preparations for the screening. The filmmaker called everyone to attention and began the event by thanking all the friends and well-wishers who attended. He drew attention to his two sons in the audience and thanked his family for their support, then ran the film, which I discuss later. After the screening, he reflected on how and why he decided to make the film in a short speech:

> I worked with audiovisual for a long time. I want to begin by talking a little bit about what I did. I wanted to show where I came from—Black, poor, from the outskirts [*periferia*]. Also, Law 10.639 gave us great support. Social education, my history, my life—the story of my life is of an individual inside a defined group. I thought about the relation between cinema and story. Whether real or not—cinema takes part in a story [*história*]. To construct a story with your own hands. The history of Blacks was told by another group—not with their own hands. They told a story that we don't believe. For someone to have roots, they need a story. And we need a story that we made and where we represent ourselves. Ninety-nine percent of the movies are made by whites. Most of the movies about Blacks are made by whites. This law [10.639] is the fruit of the Black movement. It functions as a discussion. I'm not saying anything new to the people here who think about these themes.

The law Jefferson mentions, Law 10.639, makes African and Afro-Brazilian history and culture compulsory subjects in primary school public education.

Jefferson intended for his film to assist educators with their lessons on Afro-Brazilian history and culture. Jefferson's speech documents the importance of someone in his subject position, a poor Afro-Brazilian from the city outskirts, making a film about Afro-Brazilians.

This chapter examines that ways in which three Afro-Brazilian filmmakers in São Paulo represent Blackness, Black children, and their experiences. It specifically analyzes Santos's *A Formação do Olhar* and two short films, *Cores e Botas* (Colors and boots) by Juliana Vicente and *Jennifer* by Renato Candido. These films all focus on the racialized and gendered processes of Afro-Brazilian children and adolescents learning to view themselves and others in a society that values whiteness as a visual norm, thus confirming that "vision is (as we say) a cultural construction, that is learned and cultivated, not simply given by nature" (T. Mitchell 2002: 166). The Afro-Brazilian filmmakers in this chapter materialize their vision through films that centralize young Black protagonists and their experiences with the racialized dynamics of everyday life. In seeking to tell their own stories, these filmmakers and their films centralize the process of discerning racial dynamics as a critical process for Black children as they come of age.

The filmmakers in this section drew from their own experiences as Black children as well as working with and observing young people to develop films that confer meaning onto Black children as vulnerable to the harms of racism but also capable of transcending this context to see oneself anew. Their films confer new meanings onto Black childhood and adolescence by making Black youth visible subjects and protagonists as well as considering their processes of seeing and interpreting society.

The chapter also emphasizes the importance of Afro-Brazilian people creating their own films. bell hooks argues that the importance of films is that they "not only provide a narrative for specific discourses of race, class, and sex, they provide a shared experience, a common starting point from which diverse audiences can dialogue about these charged issues" (1996: 3). By making their films, they attempt to intervene in an industry where Afro-Brazilians are disproportionately underrepresented, and they intervene in a visual terrain where Black protagonists are a rarity. As Santos's speech indicates, they understand themselves to be filling a critical gap in the dearth of Blackness in the public sphere and the narrow and stereotypical images that Afro-Brazilians play when they are represented. Their films confront their viewers with social issues of race, class, and gender, as well as present complex Black protagonists and narratives. The filmmakers and films considered in this chapter take part in a larger Black cinema scene that indexes the centrality of accessing the means of representation to tell one's own story, which I consider as a critical component of antiracist visual politics.

The films invoke the idea of the racial politics of vision in their narratives through the filmmakers' and protagonists' acts of looking and seeing. The filmmakers both materialize and represent an "oppositional gaze," which bell hooks describes as a space of agency in which Black subjects challenge power by reclaiming the gaze to mutually recognize one another and put forth visions that affirm their subjectivity (1992: 116). Jefferson Santos invokes the primacy of the visual in the title of his film, *A Formação do Olhar* (The formation of looking). The title indicates that vision is not only a natural facet of human bodily activity but is also shaped and fashioned by society and culture. The other two films, *Jennifer* and *Cores e Botas*, show how Afro-Brazilian girls' visions of themselves and their own beauty are formed in relation to a visual terrain that values whiteness and associates it with attractiveness. Taken together, these films prioritize the ways in which Black subjects navigate the mainstream racialized visual world that Afro-Brazilians have had little control in shaping. In so doing, I argue that they offer representations of racism that identify the visual structure of society that excludes Afro-Brazilians, which moves beyond the assumption that racism only occurs through interpersonal encounters thus enacting an antiracist visual politics.

Black Children in Latin American Cinema

The films in this chapter focus on Afro-Brazilian children as potential spectators and as central characters of their narratives, thus following the pattern of including children as protagonists in Latin American films (Martin 2019; Randall 2017; C. Rocha and Siminet 2014; Maguire and Randall 2018). Rachel Randall examines the representation of children in Brazilian, Colombian, and Chilean films since the adoption of children's rights discourses in 1990 (2017: xx). She finds that "in recent years, an increasing and yet uneven awareness of children's status as subjects in their own right (not just as precursors of adult development) has permeated representations of children in film in [these three] countries" (2017: xli). The films in this chapter attend to children as subjects with racial identities that are shaped in relation to media, culture, and society. In representing Black children, the films follow the historical and social patterns that Randall describes, but they also act under the aegis of racial politics and the turn to race-based policies I describe in the introduction and chapter 1. Specifically, Law 10.639 materializes many Black movement activists' concerns for Black children's ability to access historical, cultural, and national figures that reflect them. Through the mandate to include Afro-Brazilians in curricular materials the law also expresses the need to increase awareness of Black history and culture for the general populace as well. Santos referred explicitly to Law 10.639, but all three films emphasize a concern for children, and specifically Black children, in a national context marked by a turn to racial policies.

Many Afro-Brazilian filmmakers associate children with racial politics, which contributes to "the new political associations of the child in Latin American cinema" (Martin 2019: 27). Scholars have given little attention to visual representations of Black children's experiences in Brazil. Jaime Alves has examined depictions of Afro-Brazilian boyhood in the film *City of God* (*Cidade de Deus*) and found that, "by portraying the transformation of Black children into criminals[,] *City of God* naturalizes violence as a vocation embedded in Black men's character" (2014b: 325). Afro-Brazilian girls may face other challenges and stereotypes. They are particularly burdened with standards of beauty that exclude them by constructing whiteness as attractive.[1] Additionally, Afro-Brazilian girls have to contend with the gendered image of Afro-Brazilian women, and girls by extension, as natural service workers or maids (Twine 1998). The films analyzed in this chapter offer new representations of Black children that depict the ways in which constant exposure to raced and gendered representations that privilege whiteness can render Black children vulnerable to low self-esteem. They foreground the subjective experience of racism and present possible pathways toward developing a positive view of oneself through discerning racial dynamics.

The Formation of Looking

A Formação do Olhar (The formation of looking) is a documentary about the importance of film in the classroom and its use as a way of enacting Law 10.639. The film discusses how students in the classroom are taught to see or interpret the visual world and the messages about race embedded within it. Santos wanted to produce the film like a conversation, so he chose interviewees who could fulfill different roles in the discussion. Noel dos Santos Carvalho brings an academic perspective to the conversation as a sociology professor who researches the image of Afro-Brazilians in Brazilian cinema. Linguist Ana Lucia Silva Souza teaches and writes about hip-hop and the position of Afro-Brazilians in the classroom. Jeferson De and Daniel Santiago are Afro-Brazilian filmmakers who participated in Dogma Feijoada (see chapter 1); they both have produced films centering on the lives of Afro-

Brazilians, and they bring a filmmaker perspective to the conversation. Santos interviewed all four separately for his film, asking each one questions about school, cinema, and Law 10.639 and filming their responses. He then edited the scenes to appear as a conversation between the four commentators.

While *A Formação do Olhar* constructs a conversation around the use of film in the classroom, it also creates images of Afro-Brazilians by an Afro-Brazilian filmmaker. All of the commentators are Black, and thus the film also constructs an image of Afro-Brazilians discussing these issues. The very documentation of their interviews and discussions produces resistant representations of Blackness that do not conform to images already in circulation. The commentators advocate for the use of film in fulfilling the mandates of Law 10.639 due to its ability to depict images of Afro-Brazilians that deviate from the hegemonic whiteness of visual culture.[2] De gives a brief explanation of the context here, in which the majority of protagonists in Brazilian television and film are white men. *A Formação do Olhar* includes a short clip from De's film *Narciso Rap*, which he describes as depicting "what life was like for some young, urban, Blacks in the 1990s." Souza mentions that film can "link to the life of someone in the classroom, link to a text." Then she asks, "which films, which documentaries should we bring in?" Not only do the four interviewees advocate for film, but they offer brief pedagogical strategies to discuss film in the classroom, such as connecting it to a particular reading and the lives of the students watching it.

The film's scenes place the commentators in dialogue with one another about the three topics. This simulated conversation channels the director's goal for the film, which was to "provoke a discussion about the theme. About how the audiovisual is used in school, and in what form. Does it help or hinder?" For example, the filmmaker juxtaposes scenes of two interviewees commenting on the use of film in the classroom. These scenes simulate a conversation between the film's commentators by juxtaposing their commentary: In one scene, Noel dos Santos Carvalho states, "Cinema is a diversion, entertainment. If we open our hand to this, education will become entertainment." In the next scene, Ana Lucia Silva Souza seems to respond: "On the other hand, it doesn't make sense to think about a film as a book, right?" Then Carvalho is shown, saying "They don't show films in school. If the teacher enters the classroom with a film, they discuss a text, they discuss these types of representations, they discuss the context . . . now cinema in the classroom has the possibility to be very good, very interesting." The juxtaposed scenes simulate a conversation about the value of film in the classroom and the relationship between education and entertainment. Both commentators acknowledge that film can be considered entertainment, with no educational value. However, Carvalho explains that film has the capacity to educate if it is combined with a text and linked to a context.

After the film launch, I met Jefferson for an interview. Sitting at a table across from one another, I asked what attracted him to film, how he developed the film's concept, and his background. Jefferson says that he "started to use video as a form to register things, and documentary has fundamentally this essence—to register something." For Santos, documentary provides this fidelity to a conversation as it is carried out in the moment. About the use of documentary, Santos states: "I think documentary is a little bit closer ... in order to register the conversation, like we're doing right here, right? This is different from fiction. With fiction, you need minimally to know the structure, know the journey of the hero, the turning point, the epilogue. You need to know this structure. The documentary facilitates a little bit more feeling of letting you get closer. It lets you feel the conversation." Jefferson is saying that documentary allows him, as a producer, and viewers as well, to feel as if they are in a real-life conversation. In the film, he references the very conversation that he and I were having about race and his film. Having participated in conversations about racial identity, he wished for his documentary to register the forms that this discussion can take. The documentary does not require a plot, like a fictitious story—rather the conversation sustains the film's narrative.

Jefferson's experience working as a social educator informed his decision to make education a central theme in *A Formação do Olhar*. He works with adolescents to hone their learning skill sets in order to find work and stay in school. This work experience articulates with the film's concern about what young people are viewing and the messages about Black people conveyed through images. The film proposes video as a tool for educating students about Afro-Brazilian history and culture.

Jefferson produced *A Formação do Olhar* when he was finishing college, which he started ten years after high school. In the interim he experimented with video and worked in various educational initiatives, although he never formally studied video editing and film production. The idea to produce his film at the end of college stemmed from his experiences working in education, his experience with audiovisual experimentation, and his identity as Afro-Brazilian. While completing *A Formação do Olhar*, he was preparing to graduate from college, working to sustain himself and his family, and working informally on friends' and acquaintances' independent film projects.

As noted at the chapter opening, an extended conversation about the film and its context accompanied the premiere. The debate mirrored Jefferson's desire to construct through film a discussion around representations of Afro-Brazilians and the use of film in the classroom insofar as the launch party included a panel of two Afro-Brazilian doctoral students to act as discussants for the film. After Jefferson made his speech, an anthropology PhD student gave a background lecture on the history of education as part of the Black movement and the struggle to pass Law 10.639. This presentation offered background on the Black movement and the governmental interventions to achieve this law. The other graduate student, a sociology PhD student studying at a U.S. university, offered a critical commentary about the film. He described the film's interventions as bringing to the screen the "story, events, manifestations of the Black populace" and teaching students to view critically. Then he asked, "What do these Black writers and film makers do differently [from white film makers]?" The commentator then described a film he had seen in the United States on tennis shoes and how this film brought a hip-hop sensibility to filmmaking. He described this film as bringing a different aesthetic rooted in the vision of hip-hop, which the filmmaker brought to the screen. He said, "What is the possibility that the audiovisual brings? We're missing a radicality in the new generation of directors. The audiovisual brings new ways, new possibilities, new aesthetics." This commentator considered the documentary film he saw in the United States to provide a new or different aesthetic from its grounding in hip-hop music. He levied a challenge to Jefferson Santos on the basis that his aesthetic was not "radical" or different from other documentary films. The filmmaker responded: "When we propose to make an audiovisual work, besides manipulating the resource in your hand, when we get to appropriate—this is the way. For us to be sufficient, we need technical dominion. This film is very small and rustic. But this is not a reason not to include this perspective. I am not a filmmaker, I'm an educator. Other people have already produced. This film is a representation. It's a small representation of who we are."

Embedded within this exchange are different views of progressive Black aesthetics. The filmmaker did not respond directly to the idea of radicality in film. He opined that progress includes the ability of Black filmmakers to make films that tell stories about Black people. For Santos, the film's importance lies in the ability to render one's own image of one's people without the interference of others, as well as the capacity to foster dialogue about a contemporary issue. For the commentator, the film lacked a distinct visual aesthetic—something that made it different. After the panel presentations, the filmmaker opened the floor to the audience for questions and comments.

The audience continued the conversation by mounting a spirited defense of the filmmaker. One person said that the United States had a longer history of

Black film, more films produced by and about Black people, and had more of an infrastructure to support film. So it was unfair to compare what was coming out of the United States to films being produced in Brazil. Another person in the audience mentioned the conditions in which filmmakers produce their films and the preparation filmmaking requires: "I studied film and radio. You have to work, study, cook for yourself [*faz arroz e feijão*], and at the same time you want to make a film." Another person chimed in: "Besides having to cook for yourself, you have to have the basics. First produce, then watch. We need to learn the rules of cinema. You have to study everything outside of your camera—photography, audio." Audience members defended the filmmaker, saying that filmmakers must survive by working and performing day-to-day tasks, such as cooking, and to make a film one must know about other technical skills and abilities. Finally, one woman in the audience praised the film for its pedagogical possibilities. She said, "I am a teacher, and thinking about my colleagues, I think the film is very important. How can you bring in material that talks about Blacks outside of slavery? I want to use this in school." She was looking for other images of Black people, beyond slavery, and thought the film would be useful for introducing those possibilities in the classroom.

At its first screening, this film generated dynamic discourse among the attendees and presenters. People saw different values and possibilities in the film and voiced their responses to it during the designated time period. Many of their concerns centered on the conditions that filmmakers had to endure to create their movies. The audience expressed a knowledge and understanding of the difficulty for a marginalized filmmaker to make a film, and they supported his efforts. While the sociology panelist articulated his sense that the film lacked a radical aesthetic, the audience understood that when producing film in conditions without much structural support, just creating a final product that centers Black subjects and their perspectives for an audience to view is itself a radical act.

Jefferson Santos's film presents vision as something that should not be taken for granted, but rather as something that needs to be formed and taught. Interpretation can come through guidance at school or by others and is a social act that can be generated collectively through conversation, as demonstrated at the film premiere. He calls on educators to think about showing videos and movies in classes that deal with questions of race and representations of Afro-Brazilians and their history. He presents the idea that educators should think about how they will engage with video in the classroom and thus how they will teach their students to view this media and interpret the visual world around them. As a film about the role of film in classroom and racial pedagogy featuring and made by Afro-Brazilians, it acts not only as a site of interrogation but also as a site of representation itself. It encourages the viewer not only to talk about the role of cinema in the classroom, but it also prompts viewers to think about their own relationship to cinema and how they look *at* and *for* racial identities in the movies and films they watch. The conversation that Santos elicited at the screening was not only about whether cinema should be in the classroom, but about how Blackness should appear in film and about the very struggles Afro-Brazilian filmmakers face to even produce the films at all.

Black Cinema in Brazil

Afro-Brazilian filmmakers have created films and other media that they self-distribute and that tell their own stories. Black film directors have limited opportunities for making their own films for national distribution. The numbers of Afro-Brazilian filmmakers in the mass market are extremely small, evidenced by a study that found that, of films released from 2002 to 2014, only 2 percent of the directors were Black men (Candido et al. 2014).[3] None were Black women. The increased numbers of Afro-Brazilians making their own independent films is conditioned by "the increase in film funding, particularly for smaller film projects via *editais* [notices] of funding calls" (Dennison 2020: 102). Tatiana Heise categorizes Afro-Brazilian-produced film as an *alternative* group, which she finds to be "the most innovative of all the films discussed" (2012: 167). She describes the new representations they offer: "These are certainly not the first films to represent the problems faced by indigenous or Black groups, or by *favela* residents and rural workers. However, they are the first to articulate those problems in terms of a social identity that is specific to these groups, and therefore not 'national'" (167). Like Jefferson Santos and the other filmmakers discussed in this chapter, Afro-Brazilians inserting themselves into the position of filmmaker participates in antiracist visual politics by insisting on the presence of Black people in these roles. Unlike TV da Gente, which was a television network, Black cinema operates at different levels and through different configurations. It ranges from individuals deciding to make and distribute a film to film collectives and film festivals. Yet, Black cinema is a site where Afro-Brazilians can participate in and have control over the means of representation in order to tell stories from their own perspectives.

Black cinema has moved forward through the individual and collective work of Black filmmakers, actors, and producers. Individual Black filmmakers have accessed the necessary resources and training to bring their own films into existence. Filmmaker Juliana Vicente began her own film production company after working in mainstream film production. She provides an example of someone who exited mainstream media work to establish her own company where she could control production. At the time I interviewed Juliana in the artsy, bohemian neighborhood of Vila Madalena in São Paulo, her Preta Portê Films company had already produced four short films and she was in the process of shooting another film. The films her studio produced dealt mainly with social issues, and she also produced films by other Afro-Brazilian filmmakers in the city. Juliana first worked for other companies on full-length feature films to gain experience and to understand how these types of businesses functioned. The first work she did under the name Preta Portê Films was in 2007, when she filmed *Hip-Hop Week* in the Diadema neighborhood. She continued working for other businesses but in 2009 established Preta Portê Films and rented a cheap space to house her business. She said: "And I kept this space, which, truthfully, turned into a meeting and work space for my parallel projects." After winning a production contract in 2009, she resolved to work only with Preta Portê Films. Juliana's language of describing Preta Portê Films as a parallel space, or a space of relative autonomy where they had control over production, echoes other media producers in this chapter. She had to create her own space to produce films with greater racial diversity and films that tackled difficult social issues.

Individual Black filmmakers produce their own films independent of organized entities. Until 2018, a Black woman had not directed a feature-length film for national distribution, yet Black female film directors have been active in the independent short-film space.[4] Yasmin Thayná wrote and directed *Kbela* (2015), an experimental film that depicts Black women developing their identity and affirming themselves through accepting their hair texture. *Kbela* represents the challenges Black women face and their actions to overcome them, but it doesn't focus only on the individual. *Kbela* shows "Black women, together, united, collectively working for a process of mutual strengthening, in the battle to overcome the societal difficulties in which we live" (J. Oliveira 2016: 8). Thayná screened the film at Odeon Cinema in Rio de Janeiro, and *Kbela* has shown at various film festivals, including at the Rotterdam International Film Festival in 2017. Viviane Ferreira directed and wrote *O Dia de Jerusa* (*Jerusa's Day*) (2014), which depicts the relationship between histories of slavery and Black women in particular. The film is about an older Black woman named Jerusa (Léa Garcia) who encounters Sílvia (Débora Marçal), a young Black woman doing a consumer opinion survey for soap powder. For every survey question that Sílvia asks, Jerusa responds with stories from her life. For example, when Sílvia asks for Jerusa's full name, Jerusa tells her a story about her grandmother, an enslaved women who ran away from her owner and found another master who would rent her out as a washerwoman. Jerusa, whose full name is Jerusa Anunciação Mamede, shares part of her grandmother's name, Maria Jerusa Anunciação. The significance of this scene lies in its ability to convey "diverse experiences of enslavement and emancipation" (Souza and Santos 2016: 76). By focusing on the conversation and interactions between two Black women, the film centers Black women's stories and histories.

Black cinema is not only sustained by Black directors and their production teams, but film collectives and festivals have emerged to create the conditions for more film production and distribution. In 2007 Zózimo Bulbul established the Afro Carioca Film Center (Centro Afro Carioca de Cinema), which offers classes on film production and sessions to view and discuss Black films.[5] That same year, Bulbul also founded the Encontros de Cinema Negro: Brasil, África, Caribe e Outras Diásporas (Black Film Festival: Brazil, Africa, Caribbean and Other Diasporas), where Black film directors can screen their work. Attending the Panafrican Film and Television Festival of Ouagadougou in Burkina Faso inspired Bulbul to create the film festival in Brazil. Seeking to fill the void of films by and about Black people, Encontros de Cinema Negro offers a space for Black film directors to meet one another. It constitutes a significant step in the history of Black film and media in that it "made it possible to resume a discussion about the consolidation of the field of Black filmmakers in the world" (J. Oliveira 2016: 5). The festival is still running every year in Rio de Janeiro.

The Fórum Itinerante de Cinema Negro (FICINE, Itinerant Forum of Black Cinema) was created in November 2013 to form and educate audiences about Black film through film screenings, speeches, debates, and discussions (J. Oliveira 2016). It aims to form a national and international network of people interested in films created by and about Black people. FICINE offers classes where individual film directors will discuss their techniques, influences, and past work. The forum also hosts screenings of independent or commercial films made inside and outside of Brazil followed by a discussion moderated by researchers. They organize debates around a particular topic, such as representations of trans women in films. FICINE contributes to raising the visibility of Black film from Africa and the diaspora. By taking control of the camera, Black filmmakers have established a Black cinema scene in Brazil, where they can produce, screen, and discuss films that represent the complexity of Black experiences and the realities of racism, which I examine in the remaining sections.

Learning to See

The fictional films *Cores e Botas* and *Jennifer*, directed by Juliana Vicente and Renato Candido, respectively, depict the racial politics of vision through their young protagonists' practices of looking. If Santos's *A Formação do Olhar* asks how vision is formed, Juliana's and Renato's films address vision as a site of self-negation, as well as a site of self-realization and self-esteem building. *Cores e Botas* and *Jennifer* bring to the fore issues related to the racial dynamics of vision, specifically with regard to Afro-Brazilian girls. Both of the film's directors identify as Afro-Brazilian and drew from their experiences and perspectives to create their films. In this section I explore the commonalities and divergences in the films' treatment of Blackness, visuality, and Afro-Brazilian girlhood. In their focus on Afro-Brazilian girls, both films depict the dominance of whiteness in the visual world, show the protagonists dealing with the texture of their hair, and represent a narrative in which the character moves from emulating whiteness to valuing herself. The films differ in the ways they present the protagonists' family backgrounds: one girl comes from a working-class neighborhood in São Paulo, while another girl is part of a middle-class family.

Juliana Vicente's *Cores e Botas* (Colors and boots) features a young Black girl named Joana who watches *Xou da Xuxa* (Xuxa show) on television twice every day and aspires to be a *paquita*, a backup dancer for the show. ("Xuxa," or Maria da Graça Meneghel, hosted the *Xou da Xuxa*, a popular national children's television show in Brazil on TV Globo from 1986 to 1992.) *Xou da Xuxa* includes skits, features different singers, and showcases Xuxa singing and dancing with her backup dancers. When an audition for the next *paquita* takes place at her school, Joana tries out but doesn't win.

Juliana directed and produced the sixteen-minute *Cores e Botas* for her final project at film school and showed it at various film festivals in cities around Brazil and outside the country, including in Sarasota (Florida), Boston, and Havana. The film was also presented at the Brazil film festival in Toronto in 2013 along with other short films on Afro-Brazilian life.

Renato Candido's *Jennifer* follows the ways in which a Black female high school student navigates the relationships and insecurities of teenage life. Jennifer wrestles with self-understandings of her own beauty, her relationships with classmates and friends, and developing skills to become employable. Ultimately she seeks independence through work and develops a strong sense of herself as an individual with enough agency to make her way in life.

Renato studied audiovisual at the Universidade de São Paulo (USP) and earned a master's degree from the School of Communications and Arts. He wanted to become a filmmaker after watching several films and television shows and realizing that none of them touched him or were the kinds of work he wanted to see. *Jennifer* was his first film, aside from the shorter exercises he had completed as a film student. While at USP, Renato applied for and received funding to make his film. He wrote the script, cast the actresses, and directed the film.

Dominance of Whiteness

The directors of *Cores e Botas* and *Jennifer* use the figure of the child in their films as "a vehicle for protesting and highlighting injustice" related to the issue of Black racial exclusion from many spaces in Brazilian life (Martin 2019: 22). The racial dynamics of the visual terrain and the privilege accorded to whiteness are evidenced in *Cores e Botas* through the centrality of Xuxa's show. The opening scene depicts the main character, Joana, dancing and singing along to the *Xuxa* show in the morning before school. When she returns from school, she runs to her room and turns on Xuxa to continue to dance. Joana's adoration for Xuxa is apparent in the way she sways in front of the television with her pretend microphone, marching band jacket, and boots that resemble Xuxa's iconic costume.

Scholars have examined Xuxa as exemplary of the value bestowed on whiteness in the Brazilian media. Xuxa, a Brazilian of German descent, is known for her iconic blonde hair and blue eyes. Xuxa's popularity "promotes a white ideal of beauty, femininity, and success that invests whiteness with considerable power through mass mediation" (Simpson 1993: 14). Further, "every time Xuxa appears on the screen, she validates the desire for whiteness that is harbored by many and legitimized by the articulation of the national ideology of whitening" (83). Stephanie Dennison takes Xuxa's whiteness as her main focus and argues that Xuxa's very whiteness contributes to her fame and mass appeal in Brazil: "notions of whiteness and white superiority are written into Xuxa's star text through the star's relentless occupation of what [she] refers to as Brazilian 'white' spaces: children's entertainment, fashion, modeling, glamour photography, TV, cinema, business, and most recently, the law" (2013: 288).

Juliana explicitly chose to involve Xuxa's show in her film because she thought that Xuxa herself presented an image that all children wanted to emulate. Juliana described to me her idea for the film:

> In the '80s and '90s, here, almost all the girls wanted to be a *paquita* [one of Xuxa's backup dancers]. She was our reference. Everyone watched Xuxa.

And I, obviously, was one more person that wanted to be a backup dancer. So this history stayed in my head for many years, and when I was in film school this idea came to me. It came really because I was living a similar situation that had repeated during my childhood—I was the only Black woman in my college, you know. So the idea came to me to talk about this and I also thought *how can* we talk about this?

Rather than just talk about the experience of desiring inclusion in a space that does not represent you, the film visualizes it. The film registers the stark contrast between Joana, a Black girl, and Xuxa, a white woman. With their blonde or light-colored hair and light skin, the *paquitas*, Xuxa's backup dancers, resemble the star. Their uniform appearance—all standing side by side and wearing matching white boots and outfits resembling a marching-band uniform—created the backdrop that replicated and extended Xuxa's whiteness across the stage. Joana can master Xuxa's moves and clothes, yet Joana's brown skin and unruly, curly hair contrast with Xuxa and her backup dancers' smooth, blonde locks and white skin. Joana seems to want desperately to join this world as a backup dancer when she watches television, yet the conspicuous absence on the television of anyone who remotely resembles her indicates to the viewer her inability to belong on the Xuxa show. Juliana Vicente places Xuxa's show, and its tacit endorsement of whiteness as a beauty ideal, in the social context of a Black girl's world and creates a dialogue between this mainstream media text and a Black viewer.

Similar to Vicente's development of Joana, director Renato Candido constructs the character of Jennifer as a Black girl navigating a racialized world. Renato also drew from his own experiences when crafting his film and his characters. He had once joined a theater group and met a young woman whose mother was white and father was Black. He saw that she continued to be assigned inferior roles, despite her talents as an actress, and he attributed this pattern to her Afro-descendent background. This young woman inspired the character of Jennifer. In describing to me how he came up with the film *Jennifer*, Renato also mentioned the identity formation he went through in the university.

> *Jennifer* came as an attempt to discuss. We discuss Blackness, and we have this hierarchy of skin tone. How is the question of whiteness and Blackness with a girl who has Black features [*traços negros*], but with lighter skin, understand? How is it that she tries to access whiteness? Which I think is unattainable, but she's put in this society. The dominance of whiteness. You have as the ideal the love of a white guy. So how is it for Jennifer, a girl trying to deal with these issues?

Renato developed *Jennifer* to reconcile his observations of racial dynamics and the conversations around race he had in university. He wanted to explore racial dynamics from the perspective of a light-skinned, female protagonist. In Patricia Pinho's words, Jennifer is "white but not quite, that is, those men and women who, in spite of their light colored skin, have 'Black features' that 'taint' their whiteness" (2009: 40). Pinho also notes that anti-Black racism "operates in the devaluing of physical traits 'deemed Black' even in those who have lighter skin complexion, thus creating 'degrees of whiteness'" (40). As a light-skinned young woman with "Black" features, Jennifer is also subject to anti-Black racism, and she negotiates white dominance through attempts to access whiteness, then to reject it, and eventually, to affirm herself.

Hair

In their attempts to negotiate the whiteness of beauty standards in Brazil, both films' protagonists, Joana and Jennifer, turn mainly to their hair as a site of manipulation. Throughout the films, both characters express a desire to straighten their hair as part of their efforts to reach their goals. The desire to straighten their hair is informed by the aesthetic hierarchy that places more value on straight hair and whiteness. As elsewhere in the African diaspora, Brazilians hold ideas of "good" and "bad" hair. "Good" hair is seen as straight, smooth, and movable, while "bad" hair is characterized as coarse, tightly curled, and short or unable to grow. Joana aspires to be one of Xuxa's backup dancers, and Jennifer wants to be a cashier at a supermarket. Both characters believe that straight hair will make them more compatible with the image projected on television and in the supermarket.

The films acknowledge the effects that the dominance of whiteness as a beauty ideal can have on Black girls' evaluation of their own features. When Joana learns that there will be an audition for a position as a Xuxa backup dancer, she sees it as her chance to be not just a spectator but a part of the show. At home before the audition, Joana's mother finds her with yellow ribbons tied in her hair, which she is streaking with yellow paint to simulate Xuxa's long, straight, blonde hair (figure 11). Joana seems to know implicitly that her looks do not approximate those on the television, and the film has already established that her curly, unruly hair is one of the most striking aspects of her appearance. She believes that she can narrow the aesthetic gap by manipulating her hair, which would give her a shot at winning the audition. Her parents, however, make her wash the paint out of her hair.

At the audition for the Xuxa backup dancer, Joana stands in a line with other girls, many of whom are white with straight hair. The other girls and

FIGURE 11. Joana tries to change her hair color to blonde in *Cores e Botas* (2010). Directed by Juliana Vicente.

the adults running the audition continue to draw attention to Joana's aesthetic deviance from a white norm. "You don't look like a backup dancer," another girl says doubtfully to Joana as they stand in line. The woman running the auditions asks Joana, as she checks in, "Are we going to have an exotic *paquita*?" Unsurprisingly, Joana fails to qualify for the next round of auditions. The scenes of manipulating her hair and the responses from others recall Afro-Brazilian women's and girls' experiences with their hair as "everyday wounds of color," which Caldwell theorizes as "the relentless personal torment that Black women feel as a result of being judged according to anti-Black aesthetic standards" (2004: 23). Joana receives messages from television and those around her that do not affirm her appearance and communicate her inability to belong.

The film *Jennifer* also touches on themes of the stigma of Black hair and aesthetic manipulation through technological means. The film foregrounds the theme of technology in the opening shot of a computer screen, with Jennifer facing it in a classroom. As she walks around the room, the teacher tells students to develop characters for their stories. She says, "You know everything about the characters" and advises them to use details like "physical appearance, hair color, type of clothes, skin color—know the characters in detail." Jennifer switches the screen to her résumé. She types in her objective to become a cashier. Jennifer's friend interrupts her by putting a flash drive in the computer Jennifer is working on and pulling up a picture of herself. The two manipulate the picture by enlarging the friend's breasts. They post the pictures of her friend at a social networking site, while also perusing pictures of other people. The next scene shows two male students looking at pictures of Jennifer on a social networking site, where she poses bent over in a tank top, which offers a view of her cleavage.

Jennifer expresses her desire to straighten her hair for the purpose of obtaining a job as a cashier in a supermarket. Jennifer's mother works as a hair stylist in a salon where Jennifer gives manicures after school. During a conversation in the salon with her mother and the clients, Jennifer broaches the subject of taking her résumé to the supermarket to inquire about a checkout job. She also asks her mother about straightening her hair with an *escova progressiva*, a popular chemical hair straightening process in Brazil. One of the women, getting her own hair straightened, claims that Jennifer's hair will be better straightened than how it was in the past. She says, "You don't remember Jennifer's hair? When she was really little. With a Black person's hair. Now, no. It's much better." The woman is facing a mirror plastered with photos of women with straight hair. The woman whose hands Jennifer is manicuring tells her that she looks pretty the way she is. The other woman chimes in: "People, she [Jennifer] is right. The women in Dondorads [a supermarket] have straight, cute hair." Jennifer reveals that she wants her hair straightened for a party as well. But her mother resolves to not straighten her hair.

Jennifer's desire to straighten her hair is informed not only by hegemonic standards of beauty that value white features, but also ideas about "good appearance" (*boa aparência*) that Brazilians use informally as a requirement for employment. On its surface, the requirement of "good appearance" appears to refer to neat dress and grooming. However, it is a "thinly disguised discriminatory phrase" (Goldstein 2003: 60). The closer to white one's skin is, the better one's appearance. Jennifer's choice of employment encourages her attempts to access whiteness through hair manipulation and straightening.

Jennifer goes to the supermarket to submit her résumé to the supervisor, who places it at the bottom of a stack of papers in his hand. "Have you ever worked in a supermarket?" he asks. She answers, "No." She asks him if he will look at her résumé right now, and he says he will review it later. As she leaves the supermarket, she stares at the straight hair of the checkout workers, and on her way home gazes longingly at straight-hair wigs in the window of a wig shop and at white mannequins in a store window (figure 12). In the next scene, Jennifer sits at the computer at home, with a picture of herself on

FIGURE 12. Jennifer gazes through store windows in *Jennifer* (2011). Directed by Renato Candido.

which she is pasting various straight hairstyles around her face. Her mother comes into the room and speaks to her. The camera cuts to the computer screen, revealing Jennifer's image, which she has manipulated to appear with a blonde wig, illustrating "the gendered dimensions of Brazilian racism" in the way that "Black women experience their aesthetic marginalization of their construction as ugly" (Caldwell 2004: 19). Jennifer is unable to manipulate her actual bodily appearance due to her mother's refusal to allow it. She instead fulfills her desire for straight hair through the use of Photoshop on the computer.

Both films depict Black children and young women in the act of looking at images that do not include them. Deborah Martin writes that "where filmmakers wish to denounce injustice or wrong, the child's gaze is particularly useful" (2019: 24). The use of the gaze to denounce injustice may best be expressed through Karen Lury's ideas of "seeing" and "showing":

> Seeing implies certain qualities and a particular response: it is an unregulated gaze, timeless and ahistorical, it also implies fascination and a sense in which effects (what is seen) are closer to affect (what is felt). "Seeing" is the "oooh!" of wonder at fireworks in the night, or the absorbed but pointless gaze which follows ants and beetles as they labour in the grass, returns again to the scab on the knee, explores cloudy breath on a windowpane.

"Showing," in constant contrast, is precisely not this, but is a directed gaze, purposeful; it is also historical, part of a narrative which links cause to effect, it demonstrates names and classifies. (2005: 308).

Lury notes that "the 'trick' to cinema is that it presents 'showing' as 'seeing'" (309), which Martin explains as "cinema shows whilst creating the impression that we are simply 'seeing'" (2019: 8). The visual world that values straight hair is visualized in both films through the various images of Xuxa on television, straight-haired wigs in the wig shop, the white (hairless) mannequins, and photos that depict the ideal of straight hair in a beauty salon. The viewer navigates or sees the world through the subject position of a Black girl or young woman as the camera uses the subjective shot to track the vision of the main characters. Yet the camera also shows us the relation between the constant exposure to white beauty norms and both characters' perceptions of their curly hair as unacceptable. In attempting to fit into these norms, both characters wish to straighten their hair, a tactic that will move them closer to an acceptable appearance. Thus, the films use the Black girl's and young woman's gazes to depict and denounce the possible effects of a visual world that devalues Black features on young Black girls.

Family and Class

Joana and Jennifer occupy different class positions, yet they both must negotiate the hegemony of whiteness and social prejudice. Joana is from a middle-class family with a father and mother, while Jennifer comes from a working-class family in the outskirts, headed by a single mother. Joana's family lives in a nice, single-family home, employs a maid, owns a car, and both parents seem to have professional jobs evidenced by the work attire of suits and dresses. Joana has her own bedroom equipped with a television for her own viewing pleasure. Director Juliana Vicente told me that she decided to place Joana in a middle-class home in order to make the point that a middle-class family will provide her protagonist with all the possibilities in life, but there remains the limit of race. Her conscious placement of Joana challenges the long-held belief in Brazil that inequality is based more on class than race: "Because there exists a question of prejudice, if it is racial or social," she has said, "I wanted very much to talk about racial prejudice, because it still exists, independent of the social question. So in *Cores e Botas*, I put Joana in a family that was middle-class, that has all the economic opportunities. But still, this is not the solution for all of their problems. So this was the point that I wanted to discuss, and it's something we discuss very little."

Although the parents in the film are Black, and their daughter Joana is experiencing the anti-Black stigma of her appearance and hair, they choose not to discuss race with their children. After Joana attempts to alter her hair to mimic Xuxa's blonde, straight hair, her mother brings her into the dining room to show her father what she has done. Joana's mother asks her father, "This is serious. What are we going to do?" Her father responds, "Relax—it's just hair." Joana's mother seems to recognize the significance of Joana wanting blonde hair, although she does not explicitly state the racial implications of such desires. Joana's father brushes off the action as unimportant. After Joana loses the competition to become a *paquita*, the family goes out to dinner to celebrate her audition. The family has a conversation in which the parents continue to deny the role of race in Joana's loss:

MOTHER: Joana was really upset today. I seems like the audition was unfair. Do you think I should interfere?
FATHER: Interfere in what? This is nonsense.
MOTHER: Joana, I got you a gift. Open it—see if you like it.
(Joana opens a record with Xuxa on the cover.)
JOANA: Thanks mom, but I can't be a *paquita*.
FATHER: What is this, Daughter? It was just an audition.
MOTHER: Next time you will be able to. Remember, where there's a will, there's a way.
JOANA: No, Mom, I'm not blonde.
MOTHER: Who put this in your head? Look, the school has gone too far.
FATHER: You can be whatever you want, my daughter. It takes two things: hard work and a lot of luck.
BROTHER: Dad, stop! Mom! It's not a matter of luck. She won't be a *paquita*.
MOTHER: Eduardo, stop saying that in front of your sister.
BROTHER: It's like you don't even notice. We're not like that.
FATHER: Enough, Dudu.
MOTHER: You're exaggerating.
BROTHER: Am I?

The conversation recalls scholars' findings that many Afro-Brazilians do not talk about racism at home with their children. Yet, due to the pervasive silence around racism, Afro-Brazilian children may not know how to recognize racism or deal with it when they encounter it.[6] France Twine writes: "Their silence, although strategic for the purposes of retaining employment and sustaining harmonious relations with the white elite, ultimately sustains White domination. These experiences disempower Afro-Brazilian children and adolescents, who learn that their experiences with racism are a taboo subject for discussion with their parents and peers" (1998: 152–53). When relating this scene to me, Juliana said that she experienced racism at school, but her experiences went unacknowledged at home. She said that her parents went to public schools of predominately Black students, where they did not experience such blatant racism in school and so did not recognize it when their children talked about it. But her parents sent Juliana and her siblings to private schools, where they were the only nonwhite children and subject to racist behavior from their peers. She re-created this experience in *Cores e Botas*, in which the parents refuse to name the racial implications of who can and cannot be a *paquita*.

The title character of *Jennifer* lives on the working-class outskirts of São Paulo in a small house with her mother. At the end of the film, Jennifer rides her bike along the streets of her neighborhood, and her voiceover provides a meditation on her family, history, and identity:

> I am Jennifer Ferreira Lopes da Silva. I'm seventeen years old, and I'll be eighteen next month. I'm not an expert, but I know Word, PowerPoint, Excel. I like Photoshop also. I intend to go to college for computers or graphic design. At USP or another public university. I was born here in Vila Nova Cachoerinha. But I spent my infancy in Macaubas in Bahia. I lived with my mother and with my grandmother. When I was nine, I returned here, but just with my mother. Until then my mother paid for my schooling. There, only me and the cleaning woman spoke like *bahianas*. I had enormous hair, and the kids in the class always called me a *bahiana*. I came home crying with rage at my hair, at the way I talked. My mom says that our history is replete with many "no's" [*replete de muitos "nãos"*]. There in Macaubas, my grandmother did not have any way to study, but she became a teacher. It was said that my grandmother's patron saint was a demon, but her faith continued. I think in life we have this challenge: This courage to transform many "no"s into a "yes." And valorize what happens to us. Only today does this make sense to me. Of negation and negation, grandparents, great-grandparents made the foundation of the earth. They made it possible for me to have a life. And today it gives me certainty to feel strong, being who I am, existing, fighting, and affirming myself.

Jennifer describes her family's migration from Bahia to São Paulo as well as the stigma they experienced due to their regional accents. She expresses the tenacity of her mother and grandmother in working to provide better lives for themselves and their families. It is important for Jennifer to recount her background because it informs her new perspective, and recounting it inspires her to persist. Renato Candido, the filmmaker, was aware of how São Paulo's outskirts appeared in the Brazilian media, referencing such films as *Turma do Gueto* (Ghetto class) and *Cidade Alerta* (Alert city). These mass media images present the outskirts as predominantly violent. Candido grew up in the outskirts and had a different image of it. *Jennifer* came about as a desire to show the outskirts, but not through the lens of violence. Through Jennifer's monologue, he shows that people in the outskirts have a worthy history and a story to tell.

Both films place their Black protagonists within Black families and depict their interactions and relations. *Cores e Botas* presents the main character in a middle-class family to show the continued significance of race for upwardly mobile Afro-Brazilians. This film depicts the refusal to talk about race as a problem that Black children must confront. *Jennifer* depicts a working-class family in the outskirts that has a history spanning generations, with members who immigrated to the city. Yet, despite the class position of both families, both Joana and Jennifer confront similar issues of aesthetic marginalization.

Realizing Her Own Vision and Agency

At the end of both films, Jennifer and Joana gain a greater sense of themselves and their agency. Jennifer finds strength and her own identity through her family history. Her monologue closes with "and today it gives me certainty to feel strong, being who I am, existing, fighting, and affirming myself." Jennifer also seems to finds affirmation of her appearance in the song "Olhos Coloridos" (Colored eyes), sung by Sandra de Sá and written by Macau.[7] Jennifer and her friend attend the party at a classmate's house for which she wanted to straighten her hair. On entering the party, Jennifer asks the DJ to change the music to "Olhos Coloridos." She dances with a boy as this song plays but eventually finds herself alone dancing in a room full of people, exuding confidence.

Os meus olhos coloridos	My colored eyes
Me fazem refletir	Make me think
Eu estou sempre na minha	I'm always doing it my way
E não posso mais fugir	and I can no longer escape
Meu cabelo enrolado	My curly hair
Todos querem imitar	they all want to imitate
Eles estão baratinados	They are perplexed
Também querem enrolar	and also want to curl
Você ri da minha roupa	You laugh at my clothes
Você ri do meu cabelo	You laugh at my hair
Você ri da minha pele	You laugh at my skin
Você ri do meu sorriso	You laugh at my smile
A verdade é que você	The truth is that you

Tem sangue crioulo	have Black blood
Tem cabelo duro	You have thick hair
Sarará crioulo	Sarará crioulo
Sarará crioulo	Sarará crioulo
Sarará crioulo	Sarará crioulo
Sarará crioulo	Sarará crioulo
Sarará crioulo	Sarará crioulo

The lyrics affirm Blackness through the valorization of the *crioulo* with coarse or curly hair. *Crioulo* is one of "a variety of terms to denote people of dark skin color" or someone of African descent (J. Carvalho 1999: 261).[8] Brazilians employ multiple categories to describe color variations, and *sarará* refers to a specific look of light skin, freckles, coarse hair, and light eyes.[9] Sandra de Sá, the song's writer and performer, is one of several musicians who created a new sound during the 1970s that affirmed Blackness through its lyrics and images. The Brazilian journalist and music researcher Marina Xavier asserts that "'Olhos Coloridos' is a song repeated to exhaustion because it has a very strong message that affirms Black identity through the valorization of the beauty of 'hard hair,' the *sarará*" (Boeckel 2015). By dancing to this song both independently and with another person, Jennifer appears to bask in the affirmation offered by this song. She then dances with another boy, but they appear to have a disagreement. She exits the house to stand outside with her friend. Her actions at the party create a shift in the narrative, as Jennifer comes into a sense of self that valorizes her Blackness, femininity, and body. "Olhos Coloridos" marked a new theme in songs that presented "self-esteem, pride, and a sense of autonomy from the perspective of a Black Brazilians" (J. Carvalho 1999: 287). Compared to previous songs about Blackness, "Here, race relations in Brazil are viewed through a 'Black eye'" (287). The song and this scene mark a transition for Jennifer in that she moves from viewing herself as deficient in her distance from whiteness to accepting herself and valuing her own perspective.

At the end of *Jennifer*, the protagonist is an assertive young woman who can speak up for herself. She achieves her goal of working at a supermarket. One of the final scenes shows Jennifer at her cash register, staring into the distance in a daydream. A man comes up to her and says, "brown girl [*moreninha*], are you retarded?" She stares at him and says, "no . . . and if I was, you don't have the right to talk to me that way. Do you understand?" then she rings up his item. At the end of the film, Jennifer asserts herself by defending herself from others. The last scene involves her receiving a paper flower from another employee, a young Black man. She offers him a brief kiss, implying the affirmation of Blackness.

At the end of *Cores e Botas*, Joana similarly realizes her own agency, in her case, through a Polaroid camera that she finds in her parents' car. She throws away her boots and costumes, picks up the camera and begins to take her own pictures. Her act of looking at the television and digesting an image of Xuxa that she can never embody changes to a more independent vision, where she can materialize her own perspective through the camera. Her gaze moves from looking at a television that does not include her to looking at the world with her own eyes and capturing what she sees with her camera. At the end of the film, Joana exclaims to her brother, "photographers don't need boots," while she holds up the Polaroid through which she develops her own vision.

Cores e Botas and *Jennifer* demonstrate the trend in Latin American cinema to "privilege the child's experience, perspective, and agency" (Martin 2019: 25). Translating "the child's sensorium and gaze into the filmic medium" (24) helps to achieve these representations of child and adolescent agency. Jennifer dancing to "Olhos Coloridos" and Joana's materialization of her vision through her own photography enable us to view both characters as subjects and agents who act in their own lives, rather than as objects or suffering victims. All three films communicate the imperative that young Black people learn to see or discern the racial dynamics of the world and develop their own perspective of valuing oneself in the face of visual terrain that offers little affirmation.

Audience Responses and Filmmaker Challenges

It is difficult to track audience responses to many of these independent films. Yet, digital platforms offer some glimpses into how audiences respond. Over 5,800 people have watched *Jennifer* on YouTube. The film has also shown in film festivals in Canada and in Brazil. Renato offers the film on YouTube as *Filme Menina Mulher de Pele Preta* (Young woman of Black skin film). A commenter on YouTube called Guetostyle asked, "Where is the young woman with Black skin?," referring to the lightness of the main character. Candido answered him: "Calm down, Guetostyle. This is just one episode. There are four different other stories that are being tested for their viability. The scripts are ready. We're waiting for financing. This episode is about the girl with light skin. Wait for the others." Candido intended to produce four films, featuring Black women of different skin tones. At the time of our interview, he was procuring funding for his next film project. However, some commenters did identify with the film as Black women. A commenter named Marcia Vasconcelos states, "wow I loved it ... it's really like this and this has been with me also for 20 years . . . but now I assumed my Black woman identity ah! before I forget MORENINHA [little brown girl] is shit [*caralho*] !! I adored it congratulations!!!!" Maria Vasconcelos expressed identification with Jennifer and some of the experiences depicted in the film.

Independent filmmakers face many challenges in producing their work, regardless of their background. In Brazil, the disparity in the numbers of Afro-Brazilian media producers in the mainstream media industries and the amount of influence they yield forces them to produce their work in alternative venues. They create media productions and realize their visions through a disparity in economic, labor, and technological conditions relative to their white counterparts. Thus, the majority of media produced and created by Afro-Brazilians is generated in the midst of precarious conditions, as the examples of Juliana Vicente and Jefferson Santos suggest. Both filmmakers described technical problems with the equipment during filming and editing.

Juliana Vicente noted that in the course of filming *Cores e Botas*, the team inexplicably lost 50 percent of the sound: "it was caused by some problem that no sound technician in São Paulo can manage to tell me what it was." This problem with the sound caused the film to take much longer to complete, and indeed Juliana wound up dubbing the sound to complete the film. She brought in an actor from Rio de Janeiro to São Paulo to dub the missing dialogue, and the actress playing Joana had to redo her lines. Juliana told me that "the process was super arduous and I stopped and asked myself—are we going to be able to finish this film?" She continued: "It was a film that needed to be finished, you know? It was really important for us. Not just because of college, but because it was discussing a problem." They managed to dub all the sound that had been missing in order to create a seamless sound for the film.

Jefferson Santos had technical trouble with *Jennifer* as well. A problem with the camera caused the audio for one of his interviewees to be unclear. He worked on the computer editing the sound for months in order to fill in that interview. He managed to recuperate some of the sound, but when watching the film, one can hear the problems. Technical problems extended the production time for the film.

Independent Afro-Brazilian filmmakers are concretizing their own visions and materializing their own experiences through their own films. Their films offer new perspectives on the role of racism in everyday life and the subjective experience of racism expressed through encounters with visual and aesthetic norms that do not include Black people. All three of the films considered here take vision into account through the act of learning to see.

The documentary *A Formação do Olhar* implicitly asks how people should be taught to see the world. How should their interpretive faculties be trained in the classroom to evaluate the visual world? It proposes film as a medium to introduce Black history and culture as well as to hone students' interpretive capacities. The other films address how young women of African descent learn to view themselves, and they particularly examine how they view and evaluate themselves in an environment and society structured around a hegemonic standard of beauty that privileges whiteness. The young, Black, female protagonists learn to see from the television, as in Joana constantly watching Xuxa's show and hanging posters of Xuxa in her room. Jennifer learned to see through the people telling her that straight hair is better and by looking at photos of her friends and acquaintances online. From the hegemony of whiteness, they learn to see their Black features as deficiencies, specifically their hair, informing both characters' desires to straighten it. Yet, all of the films propose empowerment through vision as well. *A Formação do Olhar* proposes that children exposed to films that depict a diverse array of people can come away with positive feelings about themselves. Once Joana and Jennifer learn to realize and trust in their own visions of themselves and the world, they seem to attain positive feelings of self-esteem.

Taking control of the camera enabled the directors of these films to draw from their own life experiences when developing the themes and narratives present in their films. The films about Black girl protagonists parallel the life experiences of the directors. Both Renato Candido and Juliana Vicente struggled through school environments in which they felt they did not belong, along with the attendant discomfort from the racism they experienced. However, each director used the tools of film production to write their own story and create their own film about a racialized experience of social life. Although I place considerable emphasis on the experiences of the directors that informed their film creation, it is important to acknowledge the collaborative nature of film creation. All the directors assembled a team, relied on others for lighting, sound, and editing, and enlisted actors and commentators to enact the actual theme or script. Yet, all three films in this chapter are considered short films and produced with minimal budgets. The directors had maximum control over script writing, casting, filming, and production, which makes them central to the film's narrative. Their films address the theme of the effects of a predominately white visual world on the souls of Black and brown young people. These themes do not appear frequently in dominant Brazilian media, perhaps due to mainstream media's perpetuation of the very problem these films address. Afro-Brazilians controlling their own films can give rise to narratives that break from visions structured by traditional ideals and present subject matter that encourages the viewer to learn to see differently.

The films in this chapter made young Black people visible and central to the narrative. The directors create coming-of-age narratives that present the transition from low self-esteem to high as marked by affirmations of Blackness or the recognition of racial inequality. Rather than view Black young people as naturally violent or servants, an "oppositional gaze" attends to the structural conditions and contexts that produce Black marginality. They move beyond representations of racism as individual actions, to depict how the visual world is structured in ways that value whiteness and exclude Blackness. In these films, an "oppositional gaze" entails finding the beauty in Blackness and discerning racial dynamics, which develops from an ambiguous process of encounters, interactions, and realizations that occur in daily life. As bell hooks asserts, "In resistance struggle, the power of the dominated to assert agency by claiming and cultivating 'awareness' politicizes 'looking' relations—one learns to look a certain way in order to resist" (1992: 116). These filmmakers enlist images of Black children in the struggle over representation as sites of potential and hope for the future. Their sight lines are cast as important conduits through which to bring forth a future of critical, racially conscious subjects that can resist, call into question, transcend, or overturn racist ways of looking that exclude Black people.

Conclusion
Antiracist Visual Politics

I argue that Afro-Brazilian media and visual culture producers and their representations do antiracist work by claiming ownership or control over production, ascribing new meanings to Blackness, and representing racism beyond downplaying it or casting it as racial insults. Through their actions of media production and circulation, they foment antiracist visual politics by calling into question who gets to represent Blackness and how. Afro-Brazilian media and antiracist visual politics are not new. They are rooted in histories of past Black media production and are linked to Black activism and politics, which is foundational to the antiracist imperatives that it constitutes. Afro-Brazilian media producers offer a pathway toward possible films, videos, stories, and images that more closely approximate the complexity of Black lives in Brazil.

This book draws attention to three dimensions of antiracist visual politics. First, accessing the means of representation takes different forms. Protests, manifestos, and denunciations are acts that have called into question who has access to the means of producing mainstream and other media. These calls serve to denaturalize the dominance of white people in front of and behind the camera by uncovering the processes of exclusion that contribute to producing the dominance of one particular group in a given space. When Afro-Brazilians assume the position of filmmaker or media producer, such as Jefferson Santos, they assert their right to inhabit such spaces and cast their presence as a challenge to racial inequality. Yet, accessing spaces of media production is not always enough, demonstrated by Conceição Lourenço's inability to include her ideas when working in mainstream media. Thus, ownership and control emerge as critical sites of access. With TV da Gente and Black cinema, Afro-Brazilians have established spaces through which they can control the production of representations as well as distribute them. Establishing one's own space to create their narratives creates the conditions for greater control over production and gives rise to the potential to ascribe their own meanings to Blackness in their narratives.

Representing racism recurs throughout the media presented. Afro-Brazilian media present racism in ways that move beyond racial insult and downplaying racism to elaborate the particular forms that it takes. In *Cores e Botas* and *Jennifer*, racism structures the visual world through the exclusion of references to Blackness, and it recurs through the patterned interpolation of Black people through stereotypes. Racist ideas of Black criminality condition Black people's vulnerability to police violence, which national heroes such as Saci and everyday people experience alike. Media has been shown as central to shaping social norms and framing social problems. Thus, Afro-Brazilian media presents new ways through which to visualize racism that name the problem in its various manifestations, which can then assist in challenging it.

Finally, Afro-Brazilian media and visual culture associate Blackness with meanings that break from dominant representations. In the Afro-Brazilian media examined in this book, Black people are agents and central to the narrative, which centers their experiences, outlooks, actions, and feelings, thus adding to the complexity of images of Blackness. At TV da Gente, they were presented as authorities over their programming and as middle-class professionals, signaling their capability for leadership and demonstrating that money does not always whiten. In chapter 3, Afro-Brazilians move from the object of ridicule to agents of critique as they deploy irony and humor to call into question the denial of racism and the national appropriation of Blackness. The *Tá Bom Pra Você?* sketches endow Black people with the potential to inhabit various identities, such as maid or housewife, or as an ideal family. Black children are made visible as sites of hope for the future and experiencing a childhood in which developing self-esteem in the face of systemic racism and learning to recognize racism are critical to moving forward in their journey and reaching their goals. Mainstream media has been central to naturalizing and normalizing the invisibility of Afro-Brazilians or their appearance as marginal and static, which buttress the racist social structure. Presenting Black subjects in ways that reflect their social realities and the complexities of their lives can contribute to eroding such limiting assumptions about Black people and Black life.

My approach to this book has been shaped by literature on Black cultural politics in Brazil, racism and antiracism, and media studies. I present antiracism as a coordinated attack that directly responds to racism point by point. It is as if meanings associated with Blackness that foment racism can be countered by opposing antiracist images. Or, if Afro-Brazilians are excluded from media production, then insert them into the position. I am aware that Black people can engage in multiple activities that can challenge, negotiate, or replicate racist structures. Additionally, I do not see antiracist visual politics as a point-for-point combat, but rather as a set of questions, modes of inquiry, or processes that interrogate the relationship between one's actions and image production and racial power dynamics. As racism manifests itself differently across time and space and morphs into new structures, it remains a moving target that requires constant vigilance. The antiracist work of images is not limited to the areas and strategies that I uncover, but it can take multiple pathways and target other sites.

Much has been written about the importance of understanding the ways in which mainstream media represents Blackness in Brazil. These inquiries are ongoing and important to index the pace of change in representations and the persistence of problems. I have extended the line of inquiry around media and visual cultural production to include Afro-Brazilians and what they envision when they have relative autonomy and control over production. This topic is akin to Asian American media activism in which "battles over representation of Asian America reveal the way that activists seeking to improve that representations of Asian Americans in entertainment media are engaging in a fight for cultural citizenship, a deeper sense of belonging and acceptance within the nation that has long rejected them" (Lopez 2016: 4). It also dovetails with the ways in which digital access has afforded minoritized cultural producers a space to create their own shows (Christian 2018). I consider the antiracist work that these kinds of projects do and argue for the importance of Afro-Brazilian media to antiracist visual production.

My lens of antiracism and choices of Black representations are meant to analyze rather than confine. Afro-Brazilians are not limited to addressing topics of racism and Blackness, and I would hope that their value would not be interpreted only as such. I consider only a small slice of Afro-Brazilian media and visual culture and thus would not characterize all Afro-Brazilian media as antiracist.[1] There are numerous Black media producers in Brazil and elsewhere in Latin America who are just embarking on their first production, wrapping one of their numerous projects, or in school training to enter into the field. This work deserves attention on the part of audiences and scholars. Black and other audiences are also rich sites through which to understand how these ideas might be taken up (C. Ferreira 2018). Afro-Brazilians have the capacity to imagine themselves outside of boundaries, which is critical to producing a rich visual field.

I write from a vantage point of a desire for social change and Black inclusion. While scholars have focused on the Black movement and Black cultural politics in different areas, I center media and visual culture as a site of racial struggle. Representing racism in its myriad forms that move beyond indifference and individual insults is critical to identifying its workings and acting to dismantle it. Re-signifying Blackness to account for their potential, multiplicity, and complexity can contribute to unfixing or unsettling the hegemonic images that mainstream media sediments. I read antiracist visual politics as potentially liberating work that directs social and political action. In the final section, I turn to an updated picture of Afro-Brazilian media.

Black Media Production Going Forward

While independent Afro-Brazilian media has remained relatively marginal, new opportunities opened up to encourage more Black productions and distribute them to wider audiences. The state and private companies created initiatives to generate more films and media by Black producers. In 2012, the Ministry of Culture under the leadership of Martha Suplicy launched the *Curta Afirmativo* (Affirmative short) program, which attempted to support more Afro-Brazilian filmmakers in creating films. They would award twenty-one short films dealing with any theme with 100,000 reais and thirteen medium-length films that focused on African ancestry with 125,000 reais. Filmmakers or producers who entered a film for consideration had to self-identify as Black. Shortly after this announcement, José Carlos do Vale Madeira, a judge from the state of Maranhão, found the program to be racist because it did not include other ethnic groups and halted the program. However, at the end of 2014, the program was finally approved and opened to entries from filmmakers around the country. The Ministry of Culture chose the winners and distributed the money for a group of Afro-Brazilian filmmakers to bring their vision into existence.

In 2018, a duo of filmmakers that included an Afro-Brazilian woman, Glenda Nicácio, and Ary Rosa brought the film *Café com Canela* (Coffee with cinnamon) to a commercial release. The film features a predominantly Black cast and is set in Salvador, Bahia. Nicácio and Rosa studied film at the Federal University of the Recôncavo of Bahia and founded their own production company. Set in Bahia, the film follows various characters struggling with loss of loved ones, focusing on the friendly relationship between two women, Violeta and Margarida. Violeta helps Margarida out of her isolated life through their interactions and conversations. This film is the first commercial release by a Black woman filmmaker.

Opportunities for wider distribution are opening up as well. On November 20, 2018, the Dia da Consciência Negra (Day of Black Consciousness), the TV Brasil channel presented a lineup of short and long films directed by Black filmmakers and that featured Black protagonists and themes (Ramos 2002). The program included *Cores e Botas* (see chapter 4). Films also included *Favela Gay* (2014; Gay favela), by Rodrigo Felha, which depicts the day-to-day life of gay favela community members in Rio de Janeiro. Camila Pitanga, a well-known actress, and Beto Brant, directed *Pitanga* (2017), a documentary about Antonio Pitanga, Camila's father, also a well-known actor. They showed fictional films such as *Cinzas* (2015; Greys), directed by Larissa Fulana da Tal, which features a young, Black university student who works as a telemarketing operator to sustain himself. This broadcast distributed Black films to whoever could access the channel, which constitutes a significant departure from typical small-scale screenings and individual distribution by the director.

Questions of Black representation have only become more critical with the election of President Jair Bolsonaro in 2018. Journalists have documented his racist, sexist, and homophobic remarks, which prompt worry about the policies he will promote. In January 2019, he restructured the Ministry of Culture, which has been a critical conduit of resources to Afro-Brazilian filmmakers through, for example, the Curta Afirmativo program. At the moment, Brazil continues to shift toward recognizing racism and redressing its effects by including Afro-Brazilians in higher education. Afro-Brazilian media producers' creation of their own images calls for the mass media to catch up by taking it upon themselves to show that Black lives are complex and that this complexity is worthy of representation.

Notes

Introduction

1. The Afonso Arinos Act of 1951 made discrimination due to race or color a misdemeanor in Brazil. The Federal Constitution of 1988 included a provision classifying racism as a crime. See Machado, Santos, and Ferreira 2015 for an overview of antiracism laws in Brazil.

2. I use the term "Afro-Brazilian" to refer to people of African descent in Brazil. I use the term "Black" to refer to people of African descent. I use the term "African American" to refer to people of African descent in the United States. These terms can obscure the complexity of these populations, as well as the complexity of racial designations in Brazil and the United States. I chose the terms because of their familiarity to U.S. audiences and their relationship to Portuguese terms such as *negro*, *preto*, and *Afro-decendente*.

3. Brazil has an extensive history and presence of citizens utilizing alternative media for their own means. See Festa and Silva 1986 and Kucinski 1991 for examples of scholarship on alternative media in Brazil. For an overview of the literature on alternative media, see Levy 2018a. Levy 2018b contributes to the literature on alternative media inside and outside of Brazil by arguing for viewing Brazil's outskirts (*periferias*) as sites of media production.

4. National narratives that foreground racial mixture and downplay racism abound in Latin America and the Caribbean, not only Brazil. Scholars have examined the dynamics of mixed race nationalism in Puerto Rico (Godreau 2015); Ecuador (Rahier 2013); Peru (Golash-Boza 2011); Colombia (Wade 1995); Trinidad (Munasinghe 2002); and Mexico (Sue 2013).

5. Gilberto Freyre is considered a central figure in developing and popularizing Brazil's understanding of itself and its international reputation as a racial democracy. Yet, he did not work alone. Locating the origins of racial democracy

before Freyre, Tshombe Miles writes, "The roots of 'Racial Democracy' in Brazil do not really start with Freyre but with the abolition movement. Before slavery ended, many Brazilians already believed Brazil to be a very tolerant country" (2019: 3). Marshall Eakin finds that "the diffusion and widespread adoption of the view that Brazilians are basically one people—one race or ethnicity sharing the same key cultural traits—forged out of the collision of Native Americans, Europeans, and Africans is driven by three powerful, interacting, sometimes converging, and at times, conflicting forces—the State, media, and the people of Brazil" (2017: 79).

6. Although Brazil has an array of programming formats, scholars have labeled the telenovela as the preeminent form of popular culture in Brazil (Straubhaar 1982). Telenovelas are serial drama programs that broadcast every evening, Monday through Saturday, on Brazil's main television networks. Unlike soap operas in the United States, telenovelas run anywhere from five to eight months and eventually end. In Brazil, telenovela authors create the narrative in conversation with audience feedback as the telenovela unfolds on the air (Hamburger 2005).

7. With a total population of 190 million, 7.6 percent identified as Black (preto), 43.1 percent identified as mixed race (pardo), 47 percent identified as white, 1.1 percent identified as Asian, and less than 1 percent identified as Indian (IGBE 2010). Edward Telles has found evidence to "support collapsing the brown and Black categories into a single category since the Black-brown distinction is clearly more ambiguous than the white-nonwhite divide" (2004: 90).

8. See João Carlos Rodrigues 1988 (in Portuguese) or Stam 1997 (in English) for a full list of the archetypes and the films, theater productions, or novels in which they can be found.

9. With the ascension of many poor workers into the middle class, TV Globo and Record television network have made an effort to appeal to this new consumer population by presenting more images of favelas, albeit altered from their actual appearance. Cacilda Rêgo notes that, "in a matter of network minutes, given that telenovelas and the evening news are aired back to back, representations move from the news images of the favela as the dwelling of predominately Black violent criminals, drug dealers, and gang members to fictional images of the favela (and the urban periphery) as an almost all white working-class haven, in which residents are dignified and admirable" (2014: 106). Favelas are also sites of considerable self-representation, with people who live in them producing their own representations of their surroundings and inhabitants, which contest dominant representations (Bezerra 2017; Custódio 2017; Levy 2018b).

10. For the history of Black migration and Black political activity in São Paulo, see Butler 1998. See Andrews 1991 for racial inequalities in the São Paulo labor market.

Chapter 1. Mediating Resistance

1. See Miki 2012 for an overview of the literature on quilombos and for a historical analysis of quilombos. See French 2009 and Farfán-Santos 2016 for anthropological analyses of contemporary struggles for land titles and identities by quilombos.

2. For an analysis of gender and Afro-Brazilian women's organizing, see Caldwell 2007, McCallum 2007, C. Rodrigues and Prado 2013, Harrington 2015, and Perry 2016.

3. Covin 1996, Kraay 1998, and Dixon 2016 document the historical and contemporary forms of Black politics in Salvador, Bahia. Scholars have drawn attention to organizations such as Ilê Aiyê and Olodum and events such as Carnaval as sites of Black resistance and Black affirmation (Crook 1993; J. J. Rodrigues 1999; Tosta 2010).

4. Despite the day of emancipation from slavery falling on May 13, 1888, Black activists insisted that November 20 mark the Dia da Consciência Negra in honor of Zumbi's death. Many contemporary Black activists assert that the emancipation was false given the current conditions of exclusion that Afro-Brazilians face. In recognizing Zumbi's defense of Palmares against the Portuguese, November 20 honors Black agency in the struggle against forces that otherwise seek to dominate them. Abdias do Nascimento articulates this when he references a manifesto created by the Movimento Negro Unificado contra Discriminação Racial (MNUCDR) in 1978 (1980: 153).

5. Eduardo Silva makes a similar argument in reference to abolitionist quilombos and their influence on emancipation: "Rui Barbosa was one of the first intellectuals to affirm that the abolition of slavery was not a gift from the imperial princess regent but was won by the slaves themselves" (2007: 119).

6. Abdias do Nascimento (1914–2011) is a towering figure in the movement for Afro-Brazilian rights and representation. In addition to founding the TEN, he served as a representative and senator in the Brazilian legislature where he proposed legislation to assist the Afro-Brazilian population. While exiled, Nascimento became an accomplished painter and artist. He also founded the Afro-Brazilian Studies and Research Institute (IPEAFRO) in Rio de Janeiro.

7. See Felix 2000 for more on the Chic Show.

8. See Dunn 2016 and McCann 2004 for a history of the development of soul music in the United States and in Brazil.

9. Bulbul was preceded by Haroldo Costa and Jose Rodrigues Cajado Filho, two Black film directors during the 1940s and 1950s. However, issues of racial identity took shape through film after the 1960s. In the 1970s, Waldyr Onofre and Antonio Pitanga were Black filmmaking contemporaries of Bulbul (Carvalho 2005).

10. Leon Hirszman is part of an era of cinema called Cinema Novo (New Cinema). Cinema Novo directors produced films in the 1960s and 1970s that

focus on social inequality. Influenced by Italian neorealism and French New Wave cinema, these directors sought to tell stories with social and political themes about the working classes in Brazil.

11. Samba schools (*escolas de samba*) are found throughout neighborhoods in Rio de Janeiro, São Paulo, and other Brazilian cities. They are spaces where people gather to sing and dance samba as well as participate in other activities. During Carnaval, samba schools compete by parading with elaborate floats, ornate costumes, and their original songs. Preparations for their Carnaval performances can take months and involve coordinating large numbers of dancers and musicians.

12. See Da Costa 2014b for how these policies are playing out.

Chapter 2. TV da Gente and Controlling the Means of Media Production

1. See Gillam 2012a for other interpretations of TV da Gente programs.

2. As the middle classes continue to grow internationally, scholars increasingly examine the middle class as a category contingent on its particular cultural and historical contexts. Social scientists have recently produced several studies illuminating how middle-class subjects continuously make, remake, and negotiate their class positions through consumptive practices or political commitments (O'Dougherty 2002; Liechty 2003; Fernandes 2006; Zhang 2010).

3. See Havens (2013) for the historical context and industrial stakes in the global distribution of African American television programs. He recounts the history of the globalization of African American television to challenge long-held assumptions among network executives that these kinds of programs will not appeal to audiences outside of the United States.

4. Exchanges between Angola and Brazil are not new. See, for example, Sweet 2003 and R. Ferreira 2012 for historical flows of culture, people, and ideas between Angola and Brazil. The exchange of television programs between Brazil and Angola as well as Angola's desire for programs that resembled the population (at least phenotypically) also has a precedent. Paulina Alberto draws attention to a 1979 article in *Journegro*, a Black journal, that "lampooned the Brazilian government's attempt to export to Angola a famous children's show, *O sítio de picapau amarelo* [The yellow woodpecker ranch; based on the writings of early-twentieth-century author Monteiro Lobato], as an example of Brazil's proud Afro-European heritage, only to have the Angolan government reject it for its racist depictions of Blacks" (2011: 288).

5. See Gillam 2012b for an extended analysis of the factors contributing to the network's demise.

Chapter 3. Animating Racism

1. See Caldeira 2012 for an analysis of graffiti in São Paulo.

2. Peek and Yankah (2003) suggest that the origin of Saci could lie in the West African folkloric figure Aroni, for which Saci is a continuation in Brazil.

3. The mediated resistance to anti-Black police violence takes part amid other protests against police violence detailed by Smith (2015, 2017) and Alves (2014a, 2018).

4. See L. Rocha 2012 for an analysis of the gendered dimensions of anti-Black police violence in Brazil.

5. See, for example, Jacobs-Huey 2006, Boyer 2013, Schwarcz 2013, and Haugerud 2013 for anthropological examinations of the relationships between irony, politics, comedy, and activism.

6. See Oliveira Júnior and Vaz 2012 for additional images and interpretations of the Saci Urbano graffiti series.

7. Araujo shows that "the Brazilian slave memory has remained concealed in the public space" (2012: 115). She contends that "the absence of slavery and museums dedicated to slavery indicates how difficult it has been for the nation to deal with its slave past" (115). Brazil is beginning to acknowledge its slave heritage through creating public heritage sites. Cicalo 2013 examines the process of negotiation involved in producing a public heritage memorial of slavery in the Valongo port in Rio de Janeiro.

8. This does not mean that Afro-Brazilians do not view their culture as a source of resistance or encode it with counter-hegemonic messages. A. Azevedo (2018) argues that by preserving African rhythms and corporeality, samba music and dance constitutes a cultural practice that resists domination.

9. Digital media operates as a platform for Afro-Brazilians to more widely distribute their images and narratives. For example, Mitchell-Walthour (2018) and Gillam (2015) provide examples of Afro-Brazilians using digital media to channel long-standing activism around Black feminism and police violence.

10. Brazil has more domestic workers per capita than any other country. The norm of having a maid in Brazil is not without racial implications: "a racial pattern prevails in Brazil in which most employers are white and there is a predominance of Black women employed as maids" (Pinho and Silva 2010: 92). Domestic work is not well compensated (Lovell 1999; Goldstein 2003). The concentration of Black women in low-wage domestic work continues a pattern of labor exploitation found during slavery (Andrews 1991; Arantes 2014).

11. See Williams 2013 for a discussion of stereotypes about Black women's sexuality.

12. The term *brau* comes from the 1970s and the influence of U.S. soul music in Brazil. Sansone explains: "among young lower class Blacks the term *brau* (from brown) acquired a positive connotation, meaning the modern young Black man experimenting with the 'soul brother' style in Bahia" (2003: 123). O. Pinho

adds to this definition: "*Braus* were (are) young Black men from the outskirts [*periferia*] that reinvent a Black visuality/corporality from re-reading the North American soul 'culture' and at the same time are stigmatized by the middle class as violent, in bad taste, and hypersexualized, that is, excessively Black and excessively masculine that in a certain sense contradicts their stigmatization" (2005: 127).

13. Lázaro Ramos and Taís Araújo play a married couple on *Mister Brau* but are also married in real life. Two of the most famous Afro-Brazilian actors, they have used their voices to draw attention to and combat racism. Guaraná 2018 and Hoff 2017 give extended attention to the racial implications of each actor's star text.

Chapter 4. Independent Lenses

1. Researchers have shown beauty is far from a neutral or subjective assessment, but rather a political category that takes into account such factors as race, gender, and class. This argument emerges clearly in studies of plastic surgery in Brazil. Edmonds 2010 and Jarrín 2017 document plastic surgery patients who reject features associated with Black ancestry, such as their nose. Jarrín explores the perspective of plastic surgeons and finds that they view their work as "correcting the mistakes resulting from racial mixture. These corrections, however, always presume a higher desirability for whiter facial features, based on an aesthetic hierarchy that devalues and medicalizes non-European features, such as the diagnosable 'negroid nose'" (2017: 27). Elizabeth Hordge-Freeman shows that Black people are aware of the stigma attached to Black features by uncovering Black parents' attempts to modify their baby's appearance. They engage in a series of "racial rituals," involving pinching their baby's nose or preventing the growth of large feet in hopes of eliminating "Black-looking racial features" (2015: 45). These studies document a clear aesthetic hierarchy in which features associated with Blackness are considered ugly and devalued.

2. See Souza 2011 for essays on the use of film in implementing Law 10.639 in the classroom.

3. The small numbers of Black directors could be due to Heise's finding that the system of selecting and funding national films "favors filmmakers who have more social capital, regardless of their talent" (2012: 59).

4. Glenda Nicácio, a Black woman, and Ary Rosa directed *Café Com Canela* (Coffee with cinnamon) in 2018 with a commercial release.

5. *Carioca* is the demonym for a resident of the city of Rio de Janeiro.

6. Hordge-Freeman did find evidence of parents racially socializing their children to resist racism by instilling in their children "a concern for cleanliness and appropriate behavior" (2015: 201).

7. See Boeckel 2015 for the background of Macau, the writer of "Olhos Col-

oridos." He discusses how he wrote the song after experiencing racism at the hands of the military police.

8. The meanings of the term *crioulo* have changed over time. Dale Torston Graden offers two meanings of the term in nineteenth-century Bahia. During slavery, the term *crioulo* "meant that a slave had been born in Brazil to distinguish him or her from a slave born in Africa" (2006: xxv). After the slave trade slowed, the term referred to a Black person born in Brazil. Graden notes that "the term *crioulo* continues to be used in twenty-first-century Brazil as a pejorative word or as a racial slur" (xxv).

9. In her elucidation of race relations in Brazil, Angela Gilliam comments on the negative associations of *sarará*: "On one occasion, someone described another Brazilian woman by saying 'She's a blonde with green eyes, rather tall,' and another woman snapped in 'Blonde nothing, she's a *sarara*.' The latter word means 'mariney' (17) or 'high yellow.' By saying this, she took the woman's phenotype out of blondeness (i.e. Europeanness) into a racial definition that definitely had African mixtures and subsequent pejorative social significance" (1974: 167).

Conclusion

1. See dos Santos and Berardo 2014 for a more extensive list of films made by Afro-Brazilian women.

Works Cited

Adorno, Sérgio. 1996. "Racismo, criminalidade violenta e justiça penal: Reus brancos e negros em perspectiva comparativa." *Estudos Historicos* 18: 283–300.
Alberto, Paulina L. 2009. "When Rio Was *Black*: Soul Music, National Culture, and the Politics of Racial Comparison in 1970s Brazil." *Hispanic American Historical Review* 89(1): 3–39.
———. 2011. *Terms of Inclusion: Black Intellectuals in Twentieth-Century Brazil*. Chapel Hill: University of North Carolina Press.
Alves, Jaime Amparo. 2014a. "From Necropolis to Blackpolis: Necropolitical Governance and Black Spatial Praxis in São Paulo, Brazil." *Antipode* 46(2): 323–39.
———. 2014b. "Narratives of Violence: The White Imagination, and the Making of Black Masculinity in 'City of God.'" *CS* 13: 313–37.
———. 2018. *The Anti-Black City: Police Terror and Black Urban Life in Brazil*. Minneapolis: University of Minnesota Press.
Alves, Jaime Amparo, and João Costa Vargas. 2017. "On Deaf Ears: Anti-Black Police Terror, Multiracial Protest and White Loyalty to the State." *Identities* 24(3): 254–74.
Andrews, George Reid. 1991. *Blacks and Whites in São Paulo, Brazil, 1888–1988*. Madison: University of Wisconsin Press.
———. 1992. "Black Political Protest in São Paulo, 1888–1988." *Journal of Latin American Studies* 24: 147–71.
Appadurai, Arjun. 1996. *Modernity at Large: Cultural Dimensions of Globalization*. Minneapolis: University of Minnesota Press.
Arantes, José Tadeu. 2014. *A longa transição de escrava a empregada doméstica*. OutrasMídias https://outraspalavras.net/outrasmidias/a-longa-transicao-entre-escrava-e-empregada-domestica/. Accessed July 7, 2020.
Araujo, Ana Lucia. 2012. "Public Memory of Slavery in Brazil." In *Slavery, Memory and Identity: National Representations and Global Legacies*, edited

by Douglas Hamilton, Kate Hodgson, and Joel Quirck, 115–30. London: Pickering and Chatto.

Araújo, Emanoel. 2015. "Thirty Years of Afro-Brazilian Art." *Critical Interventions: Journal of African Art History and Visual Culture* 9(2): 149–55.

Araújo, Joel Zito. 2000. *A negação do Brasil: O negro na telenovela brasileira*. São Paulo: Editora Senac.

———. 2002. "A estética do racismo." *Mídia e Racismo*, edited by Silvia Ramos. Rio de Janeiro: Pallas.

———. 2006. "A force de um desejo—a persistência da branquitude como padrão estético audiovisual." *Revista USP* 69: 72–79.

Atton, Chris, and Nick Couldry. 2003. "Introduction." *Media, Culture and Society* 25(5): 579–86.

Azevedo, Amailton Magno. 2018. "Samba: Um ritmo negro de resistência." *Revista do Instituto de Estudos Brasileiros* 70 May/August: 44–58.

Azevedo, Maíra. 2013. "Ator Èrico Brás leva o debate para o YouTube." *A Tarde*. https://atarde.uol.com.br/digital/materias/1534697-ator-erico-bras-leva-o-debate-racial-para-o-youtube. Accessed August 11, 2021.

Baez, Jillian. 2018. *In Search of Belonging: Latinas, Media, and Citizenship*. Urbana: University of Illinois Press.

Bezerra, Kátia da Costa. 2017. *Postcards from Rio: Favelas and the Contested Geographies of Citizenship*. New York: Fordham University Press.

Biehl, João, Byron J. Good, and Arthur Kleinman, eds. 2007. *Subjectivity: Ethnographic Investigations*. Oakland: University of California Press.

Boeckel, Cristina. 2015. "Autor dos 'Olhos Coloridos' conta que música surgiu de caso de racismo." Globo, November 20, 2015.

Boyce Davies, Carole, and Babacar M'Bow. 2007. "Towards African Diaspora Citizenship: Politicizing and Existing Global Geography." In *Black Geographies and the Politics of Place*, edited by Katherine McKittrick and Clyde Woods, 14–45. Cambridge, MA: South End Press.

Boyer, Dominic. 2013. "Simply the Best: Parody and Political Sincerity in Iceland." *American Ethnologist* 40(2): 276–87.

Brambilla, Ana Maria. 2006. "Black TV Ignites Ire in Brazil." *OhmyNews*, January 16, 2006.

Brown, Jacqueline Nassy. 1998. "Black Liverpool, Black America, and the Gendering of Diasporic Space." *Cultural Anthropology* 13(3): 291–325.

Bucciferro, Justin R. 2017. "Racial Inequality in Brazil from Independence to the Present." In *Has Latin American Inequality Changed Direction?*, edited by Luis Bértola and Jeffrey Williamson, 171–94. New York: Springer.

Burdick, John. 2013. *The Color of Sound: Race, Religion, and Music in Brazil*. New York: New York University Press.

Butler, Kim D. 1998. *Freedoms Given, Freedoms Won: Afro-Brazilians in Post-Abolition São Paulo and Salvador*. New Brunswick, NJ: Rutgers University Press.

Caldeira, Teresa P. R. 2000. *City of Walls: Crime, Segregation, and Citizenship in São Paulo*. Berkeley: University of California Press.

———. 2012. "Imprinting and Moving Around: New Visibilities and Configurations of Public Space in São Paulo." *Public Culture* 24(2): 385–419.

Caldwell, Kia Lilly. 2004. "'Look at Her Hair': The Body Politics of Black Womanhood in Brazil." *Transforming Anthropology* 11(2): 18–29.

———. 2007. *Negras in Brazil: Re-Envisioning Black Women, Citizenship, and the Politics of Identity*. New Brunswick, NJ: Rutgers University Press.

———. 2017. *Health Equity in Brazil: Intersections of Gender, Race, and Policy*. Urbana: University of Illinois Press.

Campos, Luiz Augusto, Marcia Rangel Candido, and João Feres Jr. 2014. "A raça e o gênero nas novelas dos últimos 20 anos." *Grupo de Estudos Multidisciplinares da Ação Afirmativa*. http://gemaa.iesp.uerj.br/infografico/infografico3/. Accessed August 11, 2021.

Campt, Tina. 2012. *Image Matters: Archive, Photography, and the African Diaspora in Europe*. Durham, NC: Duke University Press.

Candido, Marcia Rangel, and João Feres Júnior. 2019. "Representation and Stereotypes of Black Women in Brazilian Film." *Revista Estudos Feministas* 27(2): 1–13.

Candido, Marcia Rangel, Gabriella Moratelli, Verônica Toste Daflon, and João Feres Júnior. 2014. "'A cara do cinema nacional': Gênero e cor dos atores, diretores e roteiristas dos filmes brasileiros (2002–2012)." *Textors para discussão do GEMAA (IESP-UERJ)* 6: 1–25.

Candido, Renato, dir. 2012. *Jennifer*. São Paulo: Odun Formação e Produção. www.youtube.com/watch?v=eI8u4XUPzDs. Accessed January 31, 2020.

Cano, Ignacio. 2010. "Racial Bias in Police Use of Lethal Force in Brazil." *Police Practice and Research* 11(1): 31–43.

Carrança, Flávio. 2000. "Conferência contro o racismo: Em busca de Saídas." *Revista Raça* 5(52): 88–89.

Carrança, Flávio, and Rosane da Silva Borges. 2004. *Espelho infiel: O negro no jornalismo brasileiro*. São Paulo: Imprensa Oficial.

Carter, Eli. 2018a. *Reimagining Brazilian Television: Luiz Fernando Carvalho's Contemporary Vision*. Pittsburgh: University of Pittsburgh Press.

———. 2018b. "Representing Blackness in Brazil's Changing Television Landscape: The Cases of *Mister Brau* and *O Grande Gonzalez*." *Latin American Research Review* 53(2): 344–57.

Carvalho, José Jorge de Carvalho. 1999. "The Multiplicity of Black Identities in Brazilian Popular Music." In *Black Brazil: Culture, Identity, and Social Mobilization*, edited by Larry Crook Johnson and Randal, 249–60. Los Angeles: UCLA Latin American Center Publications.

Carvalho, Noel dos Santos. 2005. "Esboço para uma história do negro no cinema brasileiro." In *Dogma Feijoada: O cinema negro brasileiro*, edited by Jeferson De. São Paulo: Imprensa Oficial.

———. 2012. "O produtor e cineasta Zózimo Bulbul—O inventor do cinema negro brasileiro." *Revista Crioula* 12.

Carvalho, Noel dos Santos, and Petrônio Domingues. 2018. "Dogma Feijoada: A invenção do cinema negro brasileiro." *Revista Brasileira de Ciencias Sociais* 33(96): 1–17.

Christian, Aymar Jean. 2018. *Open TV: Innovation Beyond Hollywood and the Rise of Web Television*. New York: New York University Press.

Chu, Henry. 2006. "A New Color in Brazil TV." *Los Angeles Times*, January 12, 2006.

Cicalo, André. 2013. "A Voice for the Past: Making 'Public' Slavery Heritage in Rio De Janeiro." *International Journal of Tourism Anthropology* 3(2): 170–83.

Collins, Patricia Hill. 1992. "Mammies, Matriarchs and Other Controlling Images." In *Feminist Philosophies: Problems, Theories, and Applications*, edited by Janet A. Kourany, James P. Sterba, and Rosemarie Tong, 119–28. Englewood Cliffs, NJ: Prentice Hall.

Costa, Haroldo. 1989. "O negro no teatro e na TV." *Estudos Afro-Asiáticos* 15: 76–83.

Covin, David. 1996. "The Role of Culture in Brazil's Unified Black Movement, Bahia in 1992." *Journal of Black Studies* 27(1): 39–55.

———. 2006. *The Unified Black Movement in Brazil: 1978–2002*. Jefferson, NC: McFarland.

Cowie, Sam. 2018. "Bahia Is Brazil's Blackest State—but You'd Never Guess It from Latest TV Soap." *Guardian*, May 18, 2018.

Crook, Larry. 1993. "Black Consciousness, Samba Reggae, and the Re-Africanization of Bahian Carnival Music in Brazil." *World of Music* 35(2): 90–108.

Custódio, Leonardo. 2017. *Favela Media Activism: Counterpublics for Human Rights in Brazil*. Lanham, MD: Lexington Books.

Da Costa, Alexandre Emboaba. 2014a. "Confounding Anti-Racism: Mixture, Racial Democracy, and Post-Racial Politics in Brazil." *Critical Sociology* 42(4–5): 495–513.

———. 2014b. *Reimagining Black Difference and Politics in Brazil: From Racial Democracy to Multiculturalism*. New York: Palgrave Macmillan.

Dávila, Arlene. 2001. *Latinos, Inc.: The Marketing and Making of a People*. Oakland: University of California Press.

De Lima, Solange Martins Couceiro. 1998. "A identitdade da personagem negra na telenovela brasileira." Relatório Fapesp.

———. 1996–97. "Reflexos do racismo à brasileiro na mídia." *Revista USP* 32: 56–65.

———. 2000–2001. "A personagem negra na telenovela brasileira: Alguns momentos." *Revista USP* 48: 88–99.

Dennison, Stephanie. 2013. "Blonde Bombshell: Xuxa and Notions of Whiteness in Brazil." *Journal of Latin American Cultural Studies: Travesia* 22(3): 287–304.

———. 2020. *Remapping Brazilian Film Culture in the Twenty-First Century*. New York: Routledge.

Dias, Kenia, and Érico Brás, dir. 2013. *Tá Bom Pra Você?* YouTube video channel. www.youtube.com/channel/UCzyBI5wiJaFJh0RF-SPzckA.

Dietrich, Elisa. 2010. "Ziraldo's *A turma do perere*: Representations of Race in a Brazilian Children's Comic." *Afro-Hispanic Review* 29(2): 143–60.

Dixon, Kwame. 2016. *Afro-Politics and Civil Society in Salvador Da Bahia, Brazil*. Gainesville: University of Florida Press.

Dornfeld, Barry. 1998. *Producing Public Television*. Princeton, NJ: Princeton University Press.

Downing, John D. H. 2001. *Radical Media: Rebellious Communication and Social Movements*. Thousand Oaks, CA: Sage.

Du Bois, W. E. B. 1990. *The Souls of Black Folk*. New York: Library of America.

Dunn, Christopher. 2016. *Contracultura: Alternative Arts and Social Transformation in Authoritarian Brazil*. Chapel Hill: University of North Carolina Press.

Eakin, Marshall C. 2017. *Becoming Brazilians: Race and National Identity in Twentieth-Century Brazil*. Cambridge: Cambridge University Press.

Edmonds, Alexander. 2010. *Pretty Modern: Beauty, Sex, and Plastic Surgery in Brazil*. Durham, NC: Duke University Press.

"Érico Brás defende cotas para seus filhos e dispara: "Não tem negro preso na Lava-Jato. Sabe por quê?" 2018. *Glamurama*, October 21, 2018. https://glamurama.uol.com.br/erico-bras-defende-cotas-para-seus-filhos-e-dispara-nao-tem-negro-preso-na-lava-jato-sabe-por-que/. Accessed April 8, 2021.

Fanon, Frantz. 1967. *Black Skin, White Masks*. New York: Grove.

Farfán-Santos, Elizabeth. 2016. *Black Bodies, Black Rights: The Politics of Quilombolismo in Contemporary Brazil*. Austin: University of Texas Press.

Feliz, João Batista de Jesus. 2000. "Chic Show e Zimbabwe e a construção da identidade nos bailes black paulistanos." Universidade de São Paulo.

Fernandes, Leela. 2006. *India's New Middle Class: Democratic Politics in an Era of Economic Reform*. Minneapolis: University of Minnesota Press.

Fernandez, James, and Mary Taylor Huber. 2001. "Introduction: The Anthropology of Irony." In *Irony in Action: Anthropology, Practice, and the Moral Imagination*, edited by James Fernandez and Mary Taylor Huber, 1–40. Chicago: University of Chicago Press.

Fernandez, Oscar. 1977. "Black Theatre in Brazil." *Educational Theatre Journal* 29(1): 5–17.

Ferreira, Ceiça. 2018. "Memórias visuais sobre mulheres negras na recepção fílmica." *Contemporanea Comunicação e Cultura* 16(2): 389–407.

Ferreira, Roquinaldo. 2012. *Cross-Cultural Exchange in the Atlantic World: Angola and Brazil during the Era of the Slave Trade*. Cambridge: Cambridge University Press.

Ferreira, Viviane, dir. 2017. *O Dia de Jerusa*. São Paulo: Odun Formação e Produção. www.youtube.com/watch?v=0RY3pkRcPiQ. Accessed January 31, 2020.

Ferreira da Silva, Denise. 1999. "The Drama of Modernity: Color and Symbolic Exclusion in the Brazilian Telenovela." In *Black Brazil: Culture, Identity, and*

Social Mobilization, edited by Larry Crook and Randal Johnson, 339–62. Los Angeles: UCLA Latin American Center Publications.

Festa, Regina, and Carlos Eduardo Lins da Silva, eds. 1986. *Comunicação popular e alternativa no Brasil*. São Paulo: Paulinas.

Figueiredo, Angela. 2010. "Out of Place: The Experience of the Black Middle Class." In *Brazil's New Racial Politics*, edited by Bernd Reiter and Gladys L. Mitchell, 51–64. Boulder, CO: Lynne Rienner.

Fontaine, Pierre-Michel, ed. 1985. *Race, Class, and Power in Brazil*. Los Angeles: Center for Afro-American Studies, University of California.

French, Jan Hoffman. 2009. *Legalizing Identities: Becoming Black or Indian in Brazil's Northeast*. Chapel Hill: University of North Carolina Press.

Fry, Peter. 1977. "Feijoada e soul food: Notas sobre a manipulação de simbolos etnicos e nacionais." *Ensaios de Opinão* 2(2): 44–47.

Gillam, Reighan. 2012a. "Resistance Televised: The TV Da Gente Television Network and Brazilian Racial Politics." In *Watching while Black: Centering the Television of Black Audiences*, edited by Beretta E. Smith-Shomade, 207–19. New Brunswick, NJ: Rutgers University Press.

———. 2012b. "The Revolution Will Be Televised: The TV da Gente Television Network in São Paulo, Brazil." PhD diss. Cornell University.

———. 2015. "'Do I Look Suspicious?' Digital Acts in Response to Police Violence against Afro-Brazilians." *CLA Journal* 58(4): 286–303.

Gilliam, Angela. 1974. "Black and White in Latin America." *Présence Africaine* 92(2): 161–73.

Gilroy, Paul. 1993. *The Black Atlantic: Modernity and Double Consciousness*. Cambridge, MA: Harvard University Press.

Ginsburg, Faye. 1991. "Indigenous Media: Faustian Contract or Global Village?" *Cultural Anthropology* 6(1): 92–112.

———. 1997. "'From Little Things, Big Things Grow': Indigenous Activism and Cultural Activism." In *Between Resistance and Revolution: Cultural Politics and Social Protest*, edited by Richard G. Fox and Orin Starn, 118–44. New Brunswick, NJ: Rutgers University Press.

Godreau, Isar P. 2008. "San Antón for TV: Gender Performances of Puerto Rican Black Folklore." *e-misférica* 5(2).

———. 2015. *Scripts of Blackness: Race, Cultural Nationalism, and U.S. Colonialism in Puerto Rico*. Urbana: University of Illinois Press.

Golash-Boza, Tanya Maria. 2011. *Yo Soy Negro: Blackness in Peru*. Gainesville: University of Florida Press.

Goldstein, Donna. 2003. *Laughter Out of Place*. Berkeley: University of California Press.

Gonzalez, Lélia. 1985. "The Unified Black Movement: A New Stage in Black Political Mobilization." In Fontaine, *Race, Class, and Power in Brazil*, 120–34.

Graden, Dale Torston. 2006. *From Slavery to Freedom in Brazil: Bahia, 1835–1900*. Santa Fe: University of New Mexico Press.

Gray, Herman. 1995. *Watching Race: Television and the Struggle for "Blackness."* Minneapolis: University of Minnesota Press.
Grijó, Wesley Pereira, and Adam Henrique Freire Sousa. 2012. "O negro na telenovela brasileira: A atualidade das representações." *Estudos em Comunicação* 11(2012): 185–204.
Guaraná, Bruno. 2018. "Taís Araújo: The Black Helena against Brazil's Whitening Television." *Black Camera* 10(1): 42–66.
Guimarães, Antonio Sèrgio Alfredo. 1995. "Racism and Anti-Racism in Brazil: A Matter of Necessity." In *Racism and Anti-Racism in World Perspective*, edited by Benjamin P. Browser, 208–26. Thousand Oaks, CA: Sage.
Hall, Stuart, ed. 1997. *Representation: Cultural Representations and Signifying Practices.* Thousand Oaks, CA: Sage.
Hamburger, Esther. 2005. *Brasil antenado: Sociedade da novela.* Rio de Janeiro: Zahar.
Hanchard, Michael. 1994. *Orpheus and Power: The Movimento Negro of Rio de Janeiro and São Paulo, Brazil, 1945–1988.* Princeton, NJ: Princeton University Press.
Harrington, Jaira J. 2015. "A Place of Their Own: Black Feminist Leadership and Economic and Educational Justice in São Paulo and Rio de Janeiro, Brazil." *Latin American and Caribbean Ethnic Studies* 10(3): 271–87.
Harris, Marvin. 1964. *Patterns of Race in the Americas.* New York: Walker.
Hasenbalg, Carlos A. 1985. "Racial and Socioeconomic Inequalities in Brazil." In Fontaine, *Race, Class, and Power in Brazil*, 25–41.
Haugerud, Angelique. 2013. *No Billionaire Left Behind: Satirical Activism in America.* Stanford, CA: Stanford University Press.
Havens, Timothy. 2013. *Black Television Travels: African American Media around the Globe.* New York: New York University Press.
Heise, Tatiana Signorelli. 2012. *Remaking Brazil: Contested National Identities in Contemporary Brazilian Cinema.* Cardiff: University of Wales Press.
Heringer, Rosana. 1995. "Introduction to the Analysis of Racism and Anti-Racism in Brazil." *Racism and Anti-Racism in World Perspective*, edited by Benjamin P. Browser, 203–7. Thousand Oaks, CA: Sage.
Hoff, Ben. 2017. "The Black Body Reframed: Lázaro Ramos and the Performance of Interracial Love." In *Stars and Stardom in Brazilian Cinema*, edited by Tim Bergfelder, Lisa Shaw, João Luiz Vieira, 227–48. New York: Berghahn Books.
hooks, bell. 1992. *Black Looks: Race and Representation.* Boston: South End Press.
———. 1996. *Reel to Real: Race, Class, and Sex at the Movies.* New York: Routledge.
Hordge-Freeman, Elizabeth. 2015. *The Color of Love: Racial Features, Stigma, and Socialization in Black Brazilian Families.* Austin: University of Texas Press.
Howe, Cymene. 2008. "Spectacles of Sexuality: Televisionary Activism in Nicaragua." *Cultural Anthropology* 23(1): 48–84.
———. 2013. *Intimate Activism: The Struggle for Sexual Rights in Postrevolutionary Nicaragua.* Durham, NC: Duke University Press.

Htun, Mala. 2004. "From "Racial Democracy" to Affirmative Action: Changing State Policy on Race in Brazil." *Latin American Research Review* 39(1): 60–89.

IGBE (Instituto Brasileiro de Geografia e Estatística). 2010. "Tabela 1379—Pessoas de 5 anos ou mais de idade, total e as alfabetizadas, por cor ou raça, segundo a situação do domicílio e a idade." https://sidra.ibge.gov.br/Tabela/1379. Accessed August 11, 2021.

Jacobs-Huey, Lanita. 2006. "The Arab Is the New Nigger." *Transforming Anthropology* 14(1): 60–64.

Jarrín, Alvaro. 2017. *The Biopolitics of Beauty: Cosmetic Citizenship and Affective Capital in Brazil*. Oakland: University of California Press.

Johnson, Ollie A. 1998. "Racial Representation and Brazilian Politics: Black Members of the National Congress, 1983–1999." *Journal of Interamerican Studies and World Affairs* 40(4): 97–118.

Joyce, Samantha Nogueira. 2012. *Brazilian Telenovelas and the Myth of Racial Democracy*. Lanham, MD: Lexington Books.

Kondo, Dorinne. 2018. *Worldmaking: Race, Performance, and the Work of Creativity*. Durham, NC: Duke University Press.

Kraay, Hendrik, ed. 1998. *Afro-Brazilian Culture and Politics: Bahia, 1790s to 1990s*. London: Routledge.

Kucinski, Bernardo. 1991. *Jornalistas e revolucionários nos tempos da imprensa alternativa*. São Paulo: Página Aberta.

La Ferrara, Eliana, Alberto Chong, and Suzanne Duryea. 2012. "Soap Operas and Fertility: Evidence from Brazil." *American Economic Journal: Applied Economics* 4(4): 1–31.

La Pastina, Antonio C., Joseph D. Straubhaar, and Lirian Sifuentes. 2014. "Why Do I Feel I Don't Belong to the Brazil on TV?" *Popular Communication: The International Journal of Media and Culture* 12(2): 104–16.

Leichty, Mark. 2003. *Suitably Modern: Making Middle-Class Culture in a New Consumer Society*. Princeton, NJ: Princeton University Press.

Leslie, Michael. 1999. "The Representation of Blacks on Commercial Television in Brazil: Some Cultivation Effects." In *Black Brazil: Culture, Identity and Social Mobilization*, edited by Larry Crook and Randal Johnson, 363–76. Los Angeles: UCLA Latin American Center Publications.

Levy, Helton. 2018a. *The Internet, Politics, and Inequality in Contemporary Brazil: Peripheral Media*. Lanham, MD: Lexington Books.

———. 2018b. "Online Self-Presentation in Brazil's Favelas: Personalising the Periphery." *First Monday*, August 2018.

Lloréns, Hilda. 2018. "Beyond blanqueamiento: Black Affirmation in Contemporary Puerto Rico." *Journal of Latin American and Caribbean Ethnic Studies* 13(2): 157–78.

Lopez, Lori Kido. 2016. *Asian American Media Activism: Fighting for Cultural Citizenship*. New York: New York University Press.

Lovell, Peggy. 1999. "Development and the Persistence of Racial Inequality in Brazil." *Journal of Developing Areas* 33(3): 395–418.

Lury, Karen. 2005. "The Child in Film and Television: Introduction." *Screen* 46(3): 307–14.

Macedo, Marcio. 2007. "Baladas black e rodas de samba da terra da goroa." *Jovens na metropole: Etnografias de lazer, encontro e sociabilidade*, edited by Jose Guilherme Cantor Magnani and Bruna Mantese de Souza, 189–224. São Paulo: Terceiro Nome.

Machado, Marta Rodrigues de Assis, Natália Neres Silva Santos, and Carolina Cutrupi Ferreira. 2015. "Legislação antirracista punitiva no Brasil: Uma aproximação à aplicação do direito pelos tribunais de justiça brasileiros." *Revista de Estudos Empíricos em Direito* 2: 60–92.

Maguire, Geoffrey, and Rachel Randall, eds. 2018. *New Visions of Adolescence in Contemporary Latin American Cinema*. New York: Palgrave Macmillan.

Martin, Deborah. 2019. *The Child in Contemporary Latin American Cinema*. New York: Palgrave Macmillan.

Martín-Barbero, Jesús. 1993. *Communication, Culture, and Hegemony: From the Media to Mediations*. Thousand Oaks, CA: Sage.

Martins, Ieda Maria. 1995. *A Cena Em Sombras*. São Paulo: Editora Prospectiva.

Martins, Sergio da Silva, Carlos Alberto Medeiros, and Elisa Larkin Nascimento. 2004. "Paving Paradise: The Road from 'Racial Democracy' to Affirmative Action in Brazil." *Journal of Black Studies* 34(6): 787–816.

Matory, J. Lorand. 2005. *Black Atlantic Religion: Tradition, Transnationalism, and Matriarchy in the Afro-Brazilian Candomblé*. Princeton, NJ: Princeton University Press.

Mayer, Vicki, Miranda J. Banks, and John Thornton Caldwell, eds. 2009. *Production Studies: Cultural Studies of Media Industries*. New York: Routledge.

McCallum, Cecilia. 2007. "Women Out of Place? A Micro-Historical Perspective on the Black Feminist Movement in Salvador Da Bahia, Brazil." *Journal of Latin American Studies* 39(1): 55–80.

McCann, Bryan. 2004. "Black Pau: Uncovering the History of Brazilian Soul." In *Rockin' Las Américas: The Global Politics of Rock in Latino/a America*, edited by Deborah Pacini Hernandez, Héctor Fernández L'Hoeste, and Eric Zolov, 68–90. Pittsburgh: University of Pittsburgh Press.

Miki, Yuko. 2012. "Fleeing into Slavery: The Insurgent Geographies of Brazilian Quilombolas (Maroons), 1880–1881." *Americas* 68(4): 495–528.

Miles, Tshombe. 2019. "Reflecting on the Legacy of Brazilian Slavery and Reimagining Afro-Brazilian Agency." *History Compass* 17(1): 1–8.

Mitchell, Jasmine. 2009. "Hip-Hop Feminist Politics in the Film Antônia." *Revista Eletrônica Literatura e Autoritarismo—Dossiê*.

———. 2020. *Imagining the Mulatta: Blackness in U.S. and Brazilian Media*. Urbana: University of Illinois Press.

Mitchell, Michael, and Charles H. Wood. 1999. "Ironies of Citizenship in Brazil: Skin Color, Police Brutality, and the Challenge to Democracy in Brazil." *Social Forces* 77(3): 1001–20.

Mitchell, W. J. T. 2002. "Showing Seeing: A Critique of Visual Culture." *Journal of Visual Culture* 1(2): 165–81.

Mitchell-Walthour, Gladys L. 2017. *The Politics of Blackness: Racial Identity and Political Behavior in Contemporary Brazil.* Cambridge: Cambridge University Press.

———. 2018. "Afro-Brazilian Women YouTubers' Black Feminism in Digital Social Justice Activism." *Interfaces Brasil/Canadá, Revista Brasileira de Estudos Canadenses* 18(3): 126–75.

Moreira, Adilson. 2019. *Racismo recreativo.* São Paulo: Pólen.

Mullings, Leith. 2005. "Interrogating Racism: Toward an Antiracist Anthropology." *Annual Review of Anthropology* 34: 667–93.

Munasinghe, Viranjini. 2002. "Nationalism in Hybrid Spaces: The Production of Impurity Out of Purity." *American Ethnologist* 29(3): 663–92.

Nascimento, Abdias do. 1980. "Quilombismo: An Afro-Brazilian Political Alternative." *Journal of Black Studies* 11(2): 141–78.

O'Dougherty, Maureen. 2002. *Consumption Intensified: The Politics of Middle-Class Daily Life in Brazil.* Durham, NC: Duke University Press.

Ohmer, Sarah S. 2016. "AfroReggae and Grupo Cultural Afro Reggae: A Study of the Early Years." In *LaVerdad: An International Dialogue on Hip Hop Latinidades*, edited by Melissa Castillo-Garsow and Jason Nichols, 276–95. Columbus: Ohio State University Press.

Oliveira, D. 2004. "Representações e estereótipos do negro na mídia." *1st Seminário Internacional Mídia E Etnia.* São Paulo: ECA-USP

Oliveira, Janaína. 2016. "'Kbela' e 'Cinzas': O cinema negro no feminino do 'Dogma Feijoada' aos dias de hoje." *AVANCA Cinema.*

Oliveira Júnior, Jorge Gonçalves de, and Thiago Vaz. 2012. "Pegadas de Saci. Ensaio etno-rapsódico a quatro mãos sobre as representações de um mito." *Cadernos de Arte e Antropologia* 1: 38–52.

Owensby, Brian. 2002. *Intimate Ironies: Modernity and the Making of Middle-Class Lives in Brazil.* Stanford, CA: Stanford University Press.

Paixão, Marcelo. 2004. "Waiting for the Sun: An Account of the (Precarious) Social Situation of the African Descendant Population in Contemporary Brazil." *Journal of Black Studies* 34(6): 743–65.

Pardue, Derek. 2008. *Ideologies of Marginality in Brazilian Hip Hop.* New York: Palgrave Macmillan.

Paschel, Tianna S. 2016. *Becoming Black Political Subjects: Movements and Ethno-Racial Rights in Colombia and Brazil.* Princeton, NJ: Princeton University Press.

Patterson, Tiffany Ruby, and Robin D. G. Kelley. 2000. "Unfinished Migrations: Reflections on the African Diaspora and the Making of the Modern World." *African Studies Review* 43(1): 11–45.

Peek, Philip M., and Kwesi Yankah, eds. 2003. *African Folklore: An Encyclopedia*. New York: Routledge.

Perry, Keisha-Khan Y. 2013. *Black Women against the Land Grab: The Fight for Racial Justice in Brazil*. Minneapolis: University of Minnesota Press.

———. 2016. "Geographies of Power: Black Women Mobilizing Intersectionality in Brazil." *Meridians: Feminism, Race and Transnationalism* 14(1): 94–120.

Pestana, Mauricio. 2001. *Racista Eu? De Jeito Nenhum!* São Paulo: Escala.

Phillips, Tom. 2005. "Brazil's First Black Television Channel Tackles Legacy of 300 Years of Slavery." *Guardian*, November 21, 2005. www.theguardian.com. Accessed April 9, 2021.

Pinho, Osmundo. 2005. "Etnografias do brau: Corpo, masculinidade e raça na reafricanização em Salvador." *Estudos Feministas* 13(1): 127–46.

Pinho, Patricia de Santana. 2009. "White but Not Quite: Tones and Overtones of Whiteness in Brazil." *Small Axe* 13(2): 39–56.

Pinho, Patricia de Santana, and Elizabeth Silva. 2010. "Domestic Relations in Brazil: Legacies and Horizons." *Latin American Research Review* 45(2): 90–113.

Pinto, Ana Flávia Magalhães. 2010. *Imprensa negra no Brasil do século XIX*. São Paulo: Selo Negro.

Porto, Mauro. 2012. *Media Power and Democratization in Brazil: TV Globo and the Dilemmas of Political Accountability*. New York: Routledge.

Rahier, Jean Muteba. 2013. *Kings for Three Days: The Play of Race and Gender in an Afro-Ecuadorian Festival*. Urbana: University of Illinois Press.

Ramos, Silvia, ed. 2002. *Mídia e racismo*. Rio de Janeiro: Pallas.

Randall, Rachel. 2017. *Children on the Threshold in Contemporary Latin American Cinema: Nature, Gender, Agency*. Lanham, MD: Lexington Books.

Rêgo, Cacilda. 2014. "Centering the Margins: The Modern Favela in the Brazilian Telenovela." In *Brazil in Twenty-First Century Popular Media: Culture, Politics, and Nationalism on the World Stage*, edited by Naomi Pueo Wood, 91–110. Lanham, MD: Lexington Books.

Reiter, Bernd, and Gladys L. Mitchell. 2008. "Embracing Hip Hop as Their Own: Hip Hop and Black Racial Identity in Brazil." *Studies in Latin American Popular Culture* 27: 151–65.

Ribeiro, Djamila. 2019. *Pequeno Manual Antirracista*. São Paulo: Companhia das Letras.

Rivero, Yeidy M. 2005. *Tuning Out Blackness: Race and Nation in the History of Puerto Rican Television* Durham, NC: Duke University Press.

———. 2006. "Channeling Blackness, Challenging Racism: A Theatrical Response." *Global Media and Communication* 2(3): 335–54.

———. 2014. "Anatomy of a Protest: *Grey's Anatomy*, Colombia's *A Corazón Abierto*, and the Politicization of a Format." In *Contemporary Latino/a Media: Production, Circulation, Politics*, edited by Arlene Dávila and Yeidy M. Rivero, 149–68. New York: New York University Press.

Rocha, Caroline, and Georgia Siminet, eds. 2014. *Screening Minors in Latin American Cinema*. Lanham, MD: Lexington Books.

Rocha, Luciane de Oliveira. 2012. "Black Mothers' Experiences of Violence in Rio de Janeiro." *Cultural Dynamics* 24(1): 59–73.

Rodrigues, Cristiano, and Marco Aurelio Prado. 2013. "A History of the Black Women's Movement in Brazil: Mobilization, Political Trajectory and Articulations with the State." *Social Movement Studies* 12(2): 158–77.

Rodrigues, João Carlos. 1988. *O negro brasileiro e o cinema*. Rio de Janeiro: Editora Globo: Fundação do Cinema Brasileiro-MINC.

Rodrigues, João Jorge Santos. 1999. "Olodum and the Black Struggle in Brazil." In *Black Brazil: Culture, Identity, and Social Mobilization*, edited by Larry Crook and Randal Johnson, 43–52. Los Angeles: UCLA Latin American Center Publications.

Rosas-Moreno, Tania Cantrell. 2011. "How and Why Brazilian Journalists (Don't) Cover Race and Class Issues." *International Communication Research Journal* 46(1–2): 44–67.

———. 2014. *News and Novela in Brazilian Media: Fact, Fiction, and National Identity*. Lanham, MD: Lexington Books.

———. 2017. "Brazilian Telenovelas and Social Merchandising." *ReVista: Harvard Review of Latin America*, November 3, 2017. https://revista.drclas.harvard.edu/book/brazilian-telenovelas-and-social-merchandising. Accessed July 21, 2020.

Rubio, Daniel A., dir. 2010. *Thiago Vaz: É o Saci Urbano!* Aver.com. YouTube. www.youtube.com/watch?v=l9ZWDEwfzW8.

Sansone, Livio. 2003. *Blackness without Ethnicity: Constructing Race in Brazil*. New York: Palgrave Macmillan.

Santos, Jacqueline Lima. 2016. "Hip-Hop and the Reconfiguration of Blackness in São Paulo: The Influence of African American Political and Musical Movements in the Twentieth Century." *Social Identities: Journal for the Study of Race, Nation, and Culture* 22(2): 160–77.

Santos, Jefferson, dir. 2014. *A Formção do Olhar*. São Paulo: CinEdu. DVD.

dos Santos, Júlio César, and Rosa Maria Berardo. 2014. "Representações cinematográficas de mulheres negras." *Representações Cinematograficas De Mulheres Negras*. Anais do VII Seminário Nacional de Pesquisa em Arte e Cultura Visual Goiania-GO. UFG, FAV.

Scheper-Hughes, Nancy. 1993. *Death without Weeping: The Violence of Everyday Life in Brazil*. Berkeley: University of California Press.

Schwarcz, Lilia K. Moritz. 2013. "The Banana Emperor: D. Pedro II in Brazilian Caricatures, 1842–89." *American Ethnologist* 40(2): 310–23.

Scott, Biljana. 2004. "Picturing Irony: The Subversive Power of Photography." *Visual Communication* 3(1): 31–59.

Scott, John, and Gordon Marshall, eds. 2015. *A Dictionary of Sociology*. 3d rev. ed. New York: Oxford University Press.

Seigel, Micol. 2009. *Uneven Encounters: Making Race and Nation in Brazil and the United States*. Durham, NC: Duke University Press.

Seminário meios de comunicação e diversidade racial. 1998. Seminário meios de Comunicação e Diversidade Racial. Câmara dos Deputados: Coordenação de Publicações.

Sheriff, Robin. 2000. "Exposing Silence as Cultural Censorship: A Brazilian Case." *American Anthropologist* 102(1): 114–32.

Silva, Eduardo. 2007. "Black Abolitionists in the *Quilombo* of Leblon, Rio de Janeiro: Symbols, Organizers, and Revolutionaries." In *Beyond Slavery: The Multilayered Legacy of Africans in Latin America and the Caribbean*, edited by Darien J. Davis, 109–22. Lanham, MD: Rowan and Littlefield.

Silva, Nelson do Valle. 1985. "Updating the Cost of Not Being White in Brazil." In Fontaine, *Race, Class, and Power in Brazil*, 42–55.

Silva dos Santos, Andreia Beatriz, and Fábio Nascimento-Mandingo. 2020. "React or Be Killed: The History of Policing and the Struggle against Anti-Black Violence in Salvador, Brazil." *Radical History Review* 137: 157–76.

Simpson, Amelia. 1993. *Xuxa: The Mega-Marketing of Gender, Race, and Modernity*. Philadelphia: Temple University Press.

Smith, Christen A. 2014. "Putting Prostitutes in Their Place: Black Women, Social Violence and the Brazilian Case of Sirlei Carvalho." *Latin American Perspectives* 41(1): 107–23.

———. 2015. "Blackness, Citizenship, and the Transnational Vertigo of Violence in the Americas." *American Anthropologist* 117(2): 384–92.

———. 2016. *Afro-Paradise: Blackness Violence and Performance in Brazil*. Urbana: University of Illinois Press.

———. 2017. "Battling Anti-Black Genocide in Brazil." *NACLA Report on the Americas* 49(1): 41–47.

Smith-Shomade, Beretta E. 2008. *Pimpin' Ain't Easy: Selling Black Entertainment Television*. New York: Routledge.

Soares, Maria Andrea dos Santos. 2012. "Look, Blackness in Brazil! Disrupting the Grotesquerie of Racial Representation in Brazilian Visual Culture." *Cultural Dynamics* 24(1): 75–101.

Sodré, Muniz. 1999. *Claros e escuros: Identitdade, povo e mídia no Brasil*. Petrópolis: Vozes.

de Souza, Edileuza Penha, ed. 2011. *Negritude, cinema e educação*. Belo Horizante: Mazza.

de Souza, Edileuza Penha, and Elen Ramos dos Santos. 2016. "O dia de Jerusa: Representações de gênero identidade, memórias e afetos." *Gênero* 17(1): 67–81.

Sovik, Liv. 2004. "We Are Family: Whiteness in the Brazilian Media." *Journal of Latin American Cultural Studies* 13: 315–25.

Stam, Robert. 1997. *Tropical Multiculturalism: A Comparative History of Race in Brazilian Cinema and Culture*. Durham, NC: Duke University Press.

Straubhaar, Joseph D. 1982. "The Development of the Telenovela as the Pre-

Eminent Form of Popular Culture." *Studies in Latin American Popular Culture* 1: 138–50.

Sue, Christina A. 2013. *Land of the Cosmic Race: Race Mixture, Racism, and Mexico*. New York: Oxford University Press.

Sue, Christina, and Tanya Golash-Boza. 2013. "'It Was Only a Joke': How Racial Humor Fuels Race-Blind Ideologies in Mexico and Peru." *Ethnic and Racial Studies* 36(10): 1577–94.

Sweet, James H. 2003. *Recreating Africa: Culture, Kinship, and Religion in the African-Portuguese World, 1441–1770*. Chapel Hill: University of North Carolina Press.

de Tavares, Julio Cesar. 2010. "Deconstructing Invisibility: Race and Politics of Visual Culture in Brazil." *African and Black Diaspora: An International Journal* 3(2): 137–46.

Telles, Edward E. 2004. *Race in Another America: The Significance of Skin Color in Brazil*. Princeton, NJ: Princeton University Press.

Thomas, Deborah A. 2004. *Modern Blackness: Nationalism, Globalization, and the Politics of Culture in Jamaica*. Durham, NC: Duke University Press.

———. 2007. "Blackness across Borders: Jamaican Diasporas and New Politics of Citizenship." *Identities* 14(1–2): 111–33.

Timberg, Bernard M., and Bob Erier. 2002. *Television Talk: A History of the TV Talk Show*. Austin: University of Texas Press.

Tosta, Antonio Luciano. 2010. "Resistance and Citizenship in the Songs of Ilê Aiyê and Olodum." *Afro-Hispanic Review* 29(2): 175–94.

Turner, Terence. 1992. "Defiant Images: The Kayapo Appropriation of Video." *Anthropology Today* 8(6): 5–16.

———. 2002. "Representation, Politics, and Cultural Imagination in Indigenous Video: General Points and Kayapo Examples." In *Media Worlds: Anthropology of New Terrain*, edited by Faye Ginsburg, Lila Abu-Lughod, and Brian Larkin, 75–89. Berkeley: University of California Press.

Twark, Jill. 2007. *Humor, Satire, and Identity: Eastern German Literature in the 1990s*. Berlin: Walter de Gruyter.

Twine, Francine Winddance. 1998. *Racism in a Racial Democracy: The Maintenance of White Supremacy in Brazil*. New Brunswick, NJ: Rutgers University Press.

Valente, Rubia R., and Brian J. L. Berry. 2017. "Performance of Students Admitted through Affirmative Action in Brazil." *Latin American Research Review* 52(1): 18–34.

Vargas, João H. Costa. 2010. *Never Meant to Survive: Genocide and Utopias in Black Diaspora Communities*. New York: Rowman and Littlefield.

Vicente, Juliana, dir. 2010. *Cores e Botas*. São Paulo: Preta Portê Filmes. www.youtube.com/watch?v=Ll8EYEygU0o&t=62s. Accessed January 21, 2020.

Wade, Peter. 1995. *Blackness and Race Mixture: The Dynamics of Racial Identity in Colombia*. Baltimore: Johns Hopkins University Press.

Warner, Kristen J. 2017. "In the Time of Plastic Representation." *Film Quarterly* 71(2): 32–37.

Williams, Erica Lorraine. 2013. *Sex Tourism in Bahia: Ambiguous Entanglements*. Urbana: University of Illinois Press.

Wortham, Erica Cusi. 2013. *Indigenous Media in Mexico: Culture, Community, and the State*. Durham, NC: Duke University Press.

Xavier, Arnaldo, and Mauricio Pestana. 1993. *Manual de sobrevivência do negro no Brasil*. São Paulo: Editora Nova Sampa Diretriz.

Zhang, Li. 2010. *In Search of Paradise: Middle-Class Living in a Chinese Metropolis*. Ithaca, NJ: Cornell University Press.

Index

Abolição, 23–24
advertisements, television, 64–67, 74
affirmative action laws, 29
African Diaspora, 34, 36, 52
Afro-Brazilian film, 75–77; audience responses and filmmaker challenges with, 98–101; Black cinema in Brazil and, 83–85; collectives and festival for, 85; examination of dominance of whiteness in, 87–89; family and class examined in, 93–96; racial politics of vision in, 86–87; by women filmmakers, 106. *See also* films, Brazilian
Afro-Brazilian media: antiracism in, 5–6; antiracist visual politics in, 2, 12, 18–19, 86–87, 103–7; background on study of, 12–14; Black media and visual culture foundations of, 19–25; double consciousness of, 41; future of, 106–7; graffiti art (*see* graffiti art); growth of, 17–18; manifesto for, 27–28; middle-class and, 46–48; Pestana's cartoons in, 69–72; *Questão de Direito* and, 41–45; racism explored in, 3–4, 55; representations of Blackness in media and, 28–29; shifting the terms of recognizing and redressing racism, 2–3; *Tá Bom Pra Você?* series on YouTube, 1–2, 61–69, 73–74, 104; TV da Gente network and (*see* TV da Gente network); who controls means of production in, 6–8
Afro-Brazilians: children in Latin American cinema, 77–78; in journalism schools, 26; representations of Blackness in media and, 8–12; as television hosts, 48–50. *See also* children, Afro-Brazilian
Afro Carioca Film Center, 85
Afroreggae, 61
Alves, Ana, 41
Alves, Jaime, 9, 78
América do Sexo, 21
Amor à Vida, 10
Angola, 36
antiracism, 5–6; TV da Gente network and, 32
antiracist visual politics, 2, 12, 18–19, 86–87, 103–7
Antônia, 10
Appadurai, Arjun, 34
Artesanato do Samba, 23
Ataíde, Graça, 28

Bando de Teatro Oludum, 61
Black activism, 18–19, 30; interrogations of mainstream media in, 25–30; late 1970s growth in, 22–23; President Cardoso and, 24; soul dances and, 21–22; TV da Gente network and (*see* TV da Gente network)
Black Entertainment Television (BET) network, United States, 32, 34–35
Black media and visual culture: abolition of slavery and, 19–20; Black films from the United States incorporated into, 22; during Brazil's authoritarian regimes, 21–22; experiences of Black actors in

film and television, 26; films in, 21, 23; foundations of, 19–25; magazines in, 24; manifesto for Black cinema, 27–28; photography in, 20; soul dances and, 21–22; Teatro Experimental do Negro (TEN) in, 20–21; television and telenovas in, 4, 5, 8–12, 25
Black National Anthem, 22
Blackness: explored in *Tá Bom Pra Você?*, 62; meanings associated with, 8–12; stereotypes of, 67–68, 74, 104
Black Panthers, 23
Black soul dances, 21–22
Bolsonaro, Jair, 107
Borges, Eliane, 29
Brant, Beto, 107
Brás, Érico. See *Tá Bom Pra Você?*
Brazil: abolition of slavery in, 17, 19–20, 23–24; affirmative action laws in, 29; authoritarian regimes in, 21–22; Black activism in, 18–19; Black cinema in, 83–85; Black feminists in, 29; Dia da Consciência Negra in, 17, 32, 107; films in (*see* films, Brazilian); images of middle-class professional workers in, 41–48; under Jair Bolsonaro, 107; legal system in, 41–45; mainstream media in, 25–30, 37–41; meanings associated with Blackness in, 8–12; media censorship in, 21; middle-class in, 46–48; police violence in, 53–54, 70–71; racial democracy of, 3; racial diversity of, 33; racism in, 2–3; São Paulo, 13–14; Secretaria de Políticas de Promoção da Igualdade Racial (SEPPIR), 35; who controls means of media production in, 6–8; World Conference against Racism and, 28–29
Brazilian National Household Survey (PNAD), 53
Bulbul, Zózimo, 23–24, 27, 85

Café com Canela, 106
Caldwell, Kia Lilly, 24, 63–64, 90
Campt, Tina, 10
Candido, Marcia Rangel, 9
Candido, Renato, 86–87, 88–89, 98, 100
Cardona, Javier, 6
Cardoso, Fernando Henrique, 24
cartoons, 69–72
Carvalho, Noel dos Santos, 78–79
censorship, 21

Centro de Documentação e Informação do Artista Negro, 26
children, Afro-Brazilian: cinema representations of, 77–78; Law 10.639 and, 29, 75–76, 77–78
Choque Cultural, 6
Cidade de Deus, 9
Cinzas, 107
City of God, 78
Cleaver, Eldridge, 23
Clube Regatas do Tietê, 22
Collins, Patricia Hill, 63
Cores e Botas, 76, 77, 98, 107; audience responses and filmmaker challenges with, 99; examination of dominance of whiteness in, 87–89; family and class examined in, 93; racial politics of vision in, 86–87
Cosby Show, The, 52
Costa Vargas, João, 54
Curta Afirmativo, 106

da Tal, Larissa Fulana, 107
De, Jeferson, 27, 78
de Figueiredo, Vera, 23
de Jesus, Carolina Maria, 21
Dennison, Stephanie, 87
de Souza, Ruth, 27
Dia da Consciência Negra, 17, 32, 107
Dia da Princesa, 35–36
Dias, Kenia. See *Tá Bom Pra Você?*
do Carmo da Silva, José, 66
double consciousness, 41
Duas Caras, 4
Durban meeting, 28–29

Emperor Jones, The, 20
Encontro da Gente, 49
Encontros de Cinema Negro, 85
Estado de São Paulo, 37

Fact of Blackness, The, 39
Fanon, Frantz, 39
Faustino, Oswaldo, 37, 40, 41
Favela Gay, 107
Felha, Rodrigo, 107
feminism, 29
Ferreira, Viviane, 84
Ferreira da Silva, Denise, 9
Festival de cinema do Recife, 27
Figueiredo, Bahia, 47–48
Filme Menina Mulher de Pele Preta, 98

films, Brazilian, 21, 23; Black children in Latin American cinema and, 77–78; experiences of Black actors in, 26; manifesto for Black cinema, 27–28; São Paulo International Short Film Festival and, 27. *See also* Afro-Brazilian film
Folha de São Paulo, A, 57
Formação do Olhar, A, 75–76, 78–83; audience responses and filmmaker challenges with, 100
Fórum Itinerante de Cinema Negro (FICINE), 85
Frente Negra Basileira (FNB), 19–20, 21
Freyre, Gilberto, 21

Geledés, 25
Gilberto, João, 41–48
Gomez, Tatiana, 66
Gonçalves, Milton, 27
Gonzalez, Lélia, 30
graffiti art: critique of racism in Brazil through, 54–55; depicting police violence, 53–54; Saci Urbano, 53, 54, 56–61
grafiteiros, 53
Grijó, Wesley Pereira, 9–10
Grupo de Trabalho Interministerial para a Valorização da População Negra, 24
Guardian, 32
Guinne, Beto, 67

hair, 22, 84, 86, 88–97, 100
Hanchard, Michael, 22, 55
Harris, Marvin, 47
Heise, Tatiana, 9, 83
Heringer, Rosana, 3
hip-hop music, 81
Hip-Hop Week, 84
Hirszman, Leon, 23
hosts, TV da Gente, 48–50
Howe, Cymene, 31
humor, 55, 65–69

institutional racism, 69–70
irony, 55, 67
Isabel, Princess, 19, 20
Isto É, 70

Jennifer, 77; audience responses and filmmaker challenges with, 98–101; examination of dominance of whiteness in, 87–89; family and class examined in, 93–96; hair as site of manipulation in, 89–93; racial politics of vision in, 86–87
Jerke, Thiago, 33
Johnson, Robert, 35
Joyce, Samantha Nogueira, 4
Judge Hatchett, 42–43
Júnior, João Feres, 9

Kbela, 84
Kondo, Dorinne, 11

Latin American cinema, representations of Afro-Brazilian children in, 77–78
Law 10.639, 29, 75–76, 77–78
legal system, Brazilian, 41–45
Lloréns, Hilda, 12
Los Angeles Times, 31, 32
Lourenço, Conceição, 37, 38–39, 48
Lury, Karen, 92–93

Macedo, Haroldo, 24
Macedo, Marcio, 14
Madeira, José Carlos do, 106
magazines, 24
mainstream media in Brazil, 25–30, 37–41
Manual de Sobrevivência do Negro no Brasil, 70–71
"Margarina Black" commercial, 64–67
Martin, Deborah, 92
Martins, Ieda, 12
Martins, Sergio da Silva, 29
Medeiros, Carlos Alberto, 29
media accountability movements, 25
Meios de Comunicação e Diversidade Racial, 25–26
Melli, Nello, 23
micro-aggressions, 64, 72
middle-class, Brazilian, 46–48
Mister Brau, 72–73
Mitchell, Charles, 53–54
Mitchell, Jasmine, 10
Motta, Zezé, 26
Moura, Paula, 36
Movimento Negro Unificado contra Discriminação Racial (MNUCDR), 22, 30
Mullings, Leith, 5–6

Narciso Rap, 78
Nascimento, Abdias do, 20
Nascimento, Elisa Larkin, 29
Nascimento-Mandingo, Fábio, 54

Negação do Brasil, A, 8, 28
Netinho (José de Paulo Neto): founding of TV da Gente by, 34–36; team assembled by, 36–37
Nicácio, Glenda, 106

O Dia de Jerusa, 84–85
O Grande Gonzalez, 74
O'Neill, Eugene, 20
oppositional gaze, 101
Owensby, Brian, 46–47

Paim, Paulo, 25
Panafrican Film and Television Festival of Ouagadougou, 85
parody, 55, 65, 66–67
Pátria Minha, 25
Pedreiro de São Diogo, 23
Pestana, Mauricio, 69–72, 73
photography, 20
Pillar, Luiz Antonio, 28–29
Pitanga, Antonio, 27, 107
Pitanga, Camila, 107
plastic representations, 11
police violence, 53–54, 70–71
Porcella, Flávio, 32–33
Porto, Mauro, 25
Preta Portê Films, 84

Quarto de despejo: Diário de uma favelada, 21
Questão de Direito, 41–46
quilombos, 17

racial democracy, 3; explored in *Tá Bom Pra Você?*, 62
racism in Brazil, 2–3; affirmative action laws to combat, 29–30; antiracist visual politics to counter, 103–6; Black activism against (*see* Black activism); Black journalists and, 37–41; depicted in mainstream media, 3–4, 72–73; depicted in public graffiti art, 54–55; employment and, 72; experiences of Black actors in film and television and, 26; explored in *Tá Bom Pra Você?*, 64; institutional, 69–70; irony, parody, and humor used to understand, 55; Mauricio Pestana on, 69–72; micro-aggressions, 64, 72; during military dictatorship, 21–22; recreational, 68; stereotypes of Blackness and, 67–68, 104

Racista, Eu!? De jeito nenhum!, 70
Randall, Rachel, 77
Recife Manifesto, 27–28
recreational racism, 68
Revista Raça, 24, 28, 37, 69
Ribeiro, Djamila, 18, 30, 51
Ribeiro, Matilde, 35
Rivero, Yeidy, 6
Rocha, Rodrigo, 67
Rodrigues, João Carlos, 9
Rosa, Ary, 106
Rosas-Moreno, Tania Cantrell, 39–40
Rousseff, Dilma, 29

Sabido, Miguel, 5
Saci Urbano, 53, 54, 56–61, 73–74
Santiago, Daniel, 78
Santos, Jefferson, 75–76, 78, 79, 82–83, 99, 103
São Paulo, 13–14, 17; International Short Film Festival in, 27
satire, 65–66
Scheper-Hughes, Nancy, 55
Scott, Biljana, 55
Secretaria de Políticas de Promoção da Igualdade Racial (SEPPIR), 35
Segunda Sol, 10
Seigel, Micol, 20
Shaft, 22
Silva, Adyel, 49, 50
Silva dos Santos, Andrea Beatriz, 54
Silva Júnior, Hédio, 42–46
Silveira da Luz, Robson, 22
slavery, abolition of, 17, 19–20, 23–24
Smith, Christen, 6, 68
Soares dos Santos, Carlos Andre, 66
soul dances, 21–22
Soul on Ice, 23
Sousa, Adam Henrique Freire, 9–10
South Africa, 71
Souza, Ana Lucia Silva, 78
Souza, Paulo Henrique, 26
Sovik, Liv, 8
stereotypes of Blackness, 67–68, 104
Subúrbia, 9
Suplicy, Martha, 106

Tá Bom Pra Você?, 1–2, 13, 54, 61–69, 73–74, 104
Tapas e Beijos, 61
Teatro Experimental do Negro (TEN), 20–21

television and telenovelas: advertisements on, 64–67; experiences of Black actors in, 26; racism depicted in, 4, 72–73; representations of Blackness in, 8–12, 25; social problems depicted in, 5; *Tá Bom Pra Você?* series on YouTube, 1–2, 13, 54, 61–69. *See also* TV da Gente network

Telles, Edward, 4, 67

TV Brasil, 107

TV da Gente network, 13, 30, 103–4; Afro-Brazilians employed by, 33; Black Entertainment Television (BET) network influence on, 34–35; challenging racial discourses, 32; double consciousness and, 41; end of, 50–51; host positions at, 48–50; images of middle-class professional workers on, 41–48; international press reviews of, 32–33; legacy of, 51–52; mission of, 31–32; Netinho (José de Paulo Neto) as founder of, 34–36; previous mainstream media experience of staff at, 37–41; *Questão de Direito* on, 41–45; team assembled to control, 36–37

TV Globo, 40, 68

TV Xuxa, 68

United States, the: Black Entertainment Television network in, 32, 34–35; Black films from, 22, 81–82; *Cosby Show* in, 52; influences on TV da Gente, 34; *Judge Hatchett* show in, 42–43

Vargas, Getúlio, 21
Vasconcelos, Marcia, 98–99
Vaz, Thiago, 53, 54, 56–61, 73
Viacom, 35
Viaduto do Chá, 22
Vicente, Juliana, 83–84, 93, 99, 100
Viera, Valdemeir, 66
Vinterberg, Thomas, 27
Von Trier, Lars, 27

Warner, Kristen, 11
Wattstax, 22
women: as filmmakers, 106; in *O Dia de Jerusa*, 84–85; racism, beauty and (see *Jennifer*); racist stereotypes of, 63–64, 74; talk shows hosted by and for, 50
Wood, James, 53–54
World Conference against Racism, 28–29

Xavier, Marina, 97
Xou da Xuxa, 86

You Don't Look Like, 6
YouTube, 1–2, 98

Zito Araújo, Joel, 8, 27, 28
Zorra Total, 68
Zumbi dos Palmares, 17

REIGHAN GILLAM is an assistant professor of anthropology at the University of Southern California.

The University of Illinois Press
is a founding member of the
Association of University Presses.

University of Illinois Press
1325 South Oak Street
Champaign, IL 61820-6903
www.press.uillinois.edu